From Wasteland
to Promised Land

Liberation Theology for a Post-Marxist World

ROBERT V. ANDELSON
JAMES M. DAWSEY

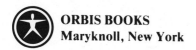

ORBIS BOOKS
Maryknoll, New York

SHEPHEARD-WALWYN
London

Library of Congress Cataloging-in-Publication Data

Andelson, Robert V., 1931-
     From wasteland to Promised Land : liberation theology for a post
-Marxist world / Robert V. Andelson, James M. Dawsey.
         p.   cm.
     Includes bibliographical references.
     ISBN 0-88344-786-X — ISBN 0-88344-793-2 (pbk.)
     1. Liberation theology.   2. Economics — Religious aspects —
Christianity.   3. Land tenure — Religious aspects — Christianity.
4. Single tax.   5. Sociology, Christian.   I. Dawsey, James M.
II. Title.
BT83.57.A52   1991
230'.046 — dc20   91-38675
                                                              CIP

British Library Cataloguing-in-Publication Data

Andelson, Robert V.
     From wasteland to promised land: liberation theology for a post-Marxist
     world.
     T. Title   II. Dawsey, James M.
     335.401
     ISBN 0-85683-133-6

To
Dr. Héctor Raúl Sandler
teacher of justice and heroic champion of human rights,
this book is dedicated with profound respect

Dr. Sandler, the leading South American exponent of the socio-economic approach advocated in this work, is professor of the philosophy of law at the University of Buenos Aires. A former air force officer, he served from 1963 to 1965 and from 1973 to 1976 as a member of the Argentine Chamber of Deputies, where his outspoken defense of human rights (especially in connection with the investigation of the murder of political prisoners) led to repeated assassination threats against him from a notorious death squad, and eventually to the bombing of his house on the day of the military coup of 1976. For a time, in order to pursue his activities as a legislator, he was obliged to travel to and from the congress building in disguise; at another time, he actually lived in the building as a refugee. Between 1976 and the restoration of constitutional government in Argentina, he taught law at the University of Mexico.

Contents

Foreword

I have been waiting for this book for thirty years.

In 1956 my wife and I started to live and work in South Africa. We immediately saw and felt the anger, pain, and frustration of the black communities. At that time, most liberal people — black and white — were hoping that black people would gradually be able to share the obvious advantages which were reserved to the whites. Get rid of racial prejudice, we thought, and blacks will have access to education, employment opportunities, and ultimately the vote that are enjoyed by the whites. Then liberation will come.

However, as we got into deeper contact with black people, and especially when we moved into rural Zululand, it became clear that these issues were only the overcoat concealing the inner body of the pain. Education and the right to vote were the currency that fitted most easily into the concepts of white liberals and church representatives. But underneath there was the real problem, the problem of land. Black people were angry, not merely because 13 percent of the population were controlling 85 percent of the land, but because the whites had come along with a totally different understanding of land tenure.

The idea that land could be owned by individuals was shocking to black Africans. The land belonged to the people, the tribe, the chief, or even God. It could no more be monopolized, bought, and sold than air could be monopolized, bought, and sold for the benefit of individual owners. Certainly land transactions could take place, but these could be only for the right to *use* land, not to *own* land itself. Black Africans had the same attitude as native Americans and Canadians, who could say to the newcomers, "You can take anything you have made or produced and you can call it your own; but you did not make the land, you cannot make it bigger or smaller; You cannot call it your property." Thus behind all the other anger in South Africa, the deepest anger was caused by an awareness of being cheated by a false understanding of human relationship to the land.

I began to feel something of the truth of all this. But I also felt quite helpless because I knew nowhere to go to anchor my initial insight into this problem or to articulate my growing criticism of the assumptions of my own culture. At this point, someone gave me a copy of an old book by Frederick Verinder called *My Neighbour's Landmark*. A simple, almost naïve book, it convinced me of three principles:

- That the primary form of wealth is not money (which is the means of exchange of wealth, not wealth in itself) but the combined power of land, labor, and learning.
- That a truly just society would be one where these three resources are fully shared and not monopolized by either minorities or majorities.
- That the basic design for this sort of society was laid down in the Bible, and that any departure from this design is a departure from basic biblical ethics. In Leviticus 25, for instance, the Mosaic law lays down how a liberated society should be organized in contrast to societies all around. Jesus and his followers picked up the Israelite language of release and redemption. They gave it a wider meaning, but they did not detach it from its basic root in economic relations.

Verinder made no secret of his indebtedness to Henry George's classic study *Progress and Poverty*. But for many years I have been hoping that someone with competence in theology, economics, and modern history would emerge to discuss the biblical vision of land and human community with critical and informed precision. *From Wasteland to Promised Land* at last supplies this need.

This book appears at just the right moment. I see this, of course, as a British citizen, but I believe that people in many other countries will see a similar set of relevancies. For a long time, many who have yearned for some alternative to "capitalist" philosophy have been drawn toward the theories and vision of Marx, but Marx has suddenly lost much of his credibility. Here is an opportunity for the teaching of Henry George to receive new and serious attention. At the same time, the kind of philosophy which led to the imposition of the Poll Tax in Britain has lost some of its credibility. Politicians are urgently looking for believable, just, and practical methods of taxation. This is exactly what Henry George offers. To take another example, Britain is surely not the only country where the affordability of housing has moved to the top of the agenda as an urgent moral and political issue. This problem has to be clarified so that it can be solved at its roots, where it is not primarily a problem of building costs but of land values. This is where Andelson's and Dawsey's interpretation of Henry George may have its most practical effect.

In the past, when I have tried to draw attention to the problems caused by our present systems of land tenure, people have assumed that I advocate full public ownership or nationalization of land, and they rightly dismissed this as unworkable, electorally impracticable, and historically discredited. But Andelson and Dawsey make it clear that what matters is not *formal ownership* but *sharing the wealth which the community creates from the land*. To accomplish this, forms of taxation need to be devised and tested that encourage sustainable development and equitable land-use for the benefit of all. This is urgent, as Andelson and Dawsey demonstrate, both in economies such as those of the North and in areas of the world such as Latin

America, where remnants of feudal land-use policies are largely responsible for wide-spread, intractable poverty.

If you look at our standard textbooks and dictionaries of ethics, you will find an extraordinary lack of interest in land tenure. This would surely shock and amaze the earlier disciples of Moses. *From Wasteland to Promised Land* is published just in time to provide a resource which Christian conscience needs to fill this gap. I hope that it will be widely claimed and studied. I hope that people competent in social ethics and economics will develop the implementation of the vision of this book, to enable practical endeavors of Christian obedience and political renewal.

John D. Davies
Bishop of Shrewsbury

Acknowledgments

Walter Rybeck was deeply involved with this book even before the genesis of its concept as a book. For it was at a meeting he arranged (at historic St. John's Episcopal Church across from the White House) that one of the authors gave a talk that was later published as a pamphlet by the Robert Schalkenbach Foundation. At a conference in England, the foundation's president, Lancaster M. Greene, gave a copy of the pamphlet to Anthony R. A. Werner, managing director of Shepheard-Walwyn (Publishers), who discerned in it the germ of an alternative approach for liberation theology. Upon completion of the second draft of the manuscript, a need was seen to render what was essentially an academic work intelligible to a wider readership. A grant from Schalkenbach, which it gives us pleasure to acknowledge, made the services of a professional editor available for this task, and that editor, happily, was Walt. His contribution, primarily a labor of love, can scarcely be overestimated. (We hasten to absolve him of responsibility for any impenetrable locutions or esoteric jargon that may yet remain; they were retained over his strenuous objections.)

The following persons read various drafts and made helpful criticisms and suggestions: Hugo Assmann, William R. Burrows, Paul Rowntree Clifford, John B. Cobb, Jr., Charles E. Curran, John C. Dawsey, George Gilmore, Ulrike Guthrie, Arthur F. McGovern, John T. Pawlikowski, T. Nicolaus Tideman, Anthony Werner, and Leland B. Yeager. We particularly wish to thank Dr. Assmann, whose severely negative response to the first draft forced us to rethink and rework thoroughly what we had done. (While we are not so naïve as to suppose that he will be satisfied with the result, we feel that we have produced a much better book because of what may be mildly termed his candor.)

We are grateful for useful bibliographical and other information supplied by Julia Bastian, James L. Busey, Robert Clancy, Steven B. Cord, Cyrus B. Dawsey III, Mason Gaffney, Frank C. Genovese, Sydney Gilchrist, C. Lowell Harriss, Alanna Hartzok, Will Lissner, Roger J. Sandilands, and Stanley and Marion Sapiro; and for extremely valuable advice from Fred Harrison. We also wish to record our appreciation for the generous hospitality and help accorded by D. A. and Phyllis Reily and by John and Joy Garrison to one of the authors and his wife during an exploratory trip they made to Brazil in preparation for the project.

Special thanks are due to Mr. Werner for his faith in this undertaking, manifested by unwavering encouragement that helped us to weather disappointments too numerous to mention. They are due equally to Dr. Burrows (managing editor of Orbis Books) for his zealous yet judicious patronage of the manuscript at Orbis.

Auburn University, through Richard Penaskovic, head of the Department of Religion, and Mary P. Richards, dean of the College of Liberal Arts, provided released time for one of the authors to finish the manuscript. Through Paul F. Parks, vice-president for research, Auburn University also provided funding to assist with secretarial expenses. Last, but certainly not least, Dixie M. Dawsey spent countless hours above and beyond the call of duty shepherding the typescript through more metamorphoses than she or we care to recollect.

1

Prologue

Hope for the Oppressed on Every Continent

Take away from me the noise of your songs;
To the melody of your harps I will not listen.
But let justice roll down like waters,
And righteousness like an ever-flowing stream.
Amos 5:23,24

The longing for the Promised Land — for liberation — is as timely as the headlines and magazine covers that marked the start of the 1990s. Latin American communities and clergy who were operating under the rubric of "liberation theology" began throwing off the yoke of oppression. In Europe the Berlin Wall toppled, as did seemingly well-entrenched regimes behind the formerly solid Iron Curtain.

Uprisings of subjected peoples in all corners of the earth lend immediacy to deciding what genuine liberation means. As people address this theme, they tend to emphasize *political* matters. What parties shall be permitted? How soon shall elections be conducted? Under what rules? What governmental forms shall prevail? These are all unquestionably important.

At least equally critical, however, are the *ethical* and *economic* underpinnings of liberation. These issues, which are in danger of being glossed over at the very time they are in greatest need of closer examination, are the grist for this book.

The heady feeling of breaking out of bondage can all too easily turn sour. If a new era does not incorporate elements of the good life that the oppressed had harbored in their hearts, initial elation gives way to disillusionment. Tragically, people begin to question whether the enormous sacrifices they made to chart new courses were worth the effort.

Beneath All, the Land Problem

To avert a backlash of despair, attention must focus on one of the over-arching needs of our troubled world: putting a stop to letting a relative few deprive the mass of human beings of their fair share of God's earth. "The most pressing cause of the abject poverty which millions of people in this world endure is that a mere 2.5% of landowners with more than 100 hectares control nearly three quarters of all the land in the world—with the top 0.23% controlling over half."[1] This social plague occurs in varying degrees in most of the inhabited globe. To recognize this and to respond with adequate correctives requires a clearer understanding of two great themes: the *Promised Land* and the *Wasteland*.

Think of the Promised Land as liberation, a realm of social equity and freedom, where people live in harmony with their environment and at peace with one another. The Wasteland, in contrast, is marked by chaos, by great social inequities, and by the abuse of nature's resources.

Some people in the Wasteland are so beaten down that, understandably, they view the Promised Land as an idle dream beyond the realm of the possible. This is why the freedom struggles of Chinese, Poles, Latin Americans, Romanians, Lithuanians, black South Africans, Kurds, and others can send such resonant shock waves throughout the world. Their heroic actions remind us that somehow, despite overabundant justification for hopelessness, the human spirit valiantly clings to a vision of better times.

The Promised Land is the hope of the landless. Literally, *land,* as the gateway to opportunity, is what landless people hope for: Abraham in Mesopotamia and the Israelites in bondage in Egypt so wished for their own soil that they left homes and familiar surroundings in peril of death to seek the distant place God had promised, a land rich in milk and honey where a day's labor would put food on the table and allow their children to grow into adulthood.

Not unique to biblical times, this exodus pattern has been repeated over and over, from the migrations of prehistory to the "boat people" of our day. For centuries, Europeans and then others have poured into the Americas, looking for their inheritance that had been denied them in the Old World—their portion of land.

But the Promised Land is not so much a geographic place as it is a hope and a vision—the hope and vision of a just social order. Modern society has wondrous features, spiritual as well as physical. But only the smug who blot out the unhappier features of the world around them and who mentally twist the Promised Land into something less than it should be would claim that we have yet seen its full glory. We are "modern captives" who sense the Promised Land as a primitive instinct, as a deep longing that the world should be different. It is what we cry for from the depths of captivity.

Since institutional slavery is outlawed, in what sense may one point to the "captivity" of modern man, in Europe and in the Americas, for example? All of us, like the Hebrews in Egypt, are captives of structures imposed upon us. This is more than a figure of speech. To enslave people, today as three thousand years ago, is to rob them of the value of their labor.

Millions of working people living in severe poverty are robbed of the fruits of their labor.[2] Through various forms of exploitation, and most especially through monopolization of land rights,[3] large segments of humanity are oppressed, dehumanized, held in bondage. There are many reasons why governments legalize land theft and lend respectability to exploitive landlordism. But it seems evident that one factor enabling governments to "go along" with land tenure arrangements that deprive labor of its rightful earnings has been the general silence of religious and intellectual leaders about humanity's common rights to land.

We begin to penetrate and overcome this silence when we recognize that the Wasteland is wasted land. It is unfulfilled potential, producing no "milk and honey." Speculators, in cities no less than in farm areas, keep out of use land on which the hungry, the homeless, and the jobless could feed, shelter, and employ themselves. These idle lands cause artificial shortages that drive up rents which poor people must pay for poor land. Land hoarding deserves much of the blame for creating the Wasteland: it forces people into the "desert." And what do the people find there? More land monopolists who control the oases and who must be paid a ransom in order to obtain nature's life-sustaining water.

Though part desert, there are towns and pastures in the *midbar*, the biblical Wasteland.[4] While not devoid of life, the Wasteland lacks the "fullness of life." This anomaly is mirrored in the modern Wasteland, crowded as it is with mansions, factories, skyscrapers — along with ugly blight and squalid slums. Qualitatively different from the Promised Land, too much of today's world lacks the fullness of life. This is evident not only to the poverty-stricken but to all who are offended by injustice.

The Wasteland is, or may be, a passageway. Thus, the Israelites fled from Egypt to the Wasteland and eked out a subsistence there for forty years, all the while longing for the day when they were to cross the Jordan and become caretakers of their birthright, the land which God had promised.

The Rise of Liberation Theology

This longing for the Promised Land is something of our age also. It is a ground swell in Third World countries. More than most North Americans realize, this has been fanned by what has been called the most significant theological development of the past generation, namely, liberation theology.

Before certain facets of liberation theology are held up to critical scrutiny, let the praiseworthy central core of the movement be underscored.

Liberation theologians could not abide the tendency of established religion to align itself with the wealthy and powerful. Liberation theology dared to champion the dispossessed and to brave the death squads of their oppressors. Liberation theology in several decades has made a tremendous contribution—dramatizing horrors and inequities of the modern Wasteland and reviving the passionate pursuit of the Promised Land here and now.

The point of departure of liberation theology is recognition of the awful fact that millions lead subhuman lives. The landless of rural regions seek escape in cities, often becoming squatters in *barrios* or *favelas* with open sewage and no safe water supply. They may earn fifteen dollars a month if they find work at all. Their children live in the streets and go to bed hungry. Illness and drought, and even complaining of their lot, may lead to premature death.

The landless can see the Mercedes in the driveways of the rich by peeking through the iron gates of the walled mansions. (Ironically, *mercedes* is also a Spanish legal term denoting title to a large grant of land.) The existence of these deprived people approximates that of the poor man Lazarus in Jesus' parable (Luke 16:19–31). They are the beggars, full of sores and licked by dogs, who hope to be fed with the crumbs that fall from rich men's tables. Of course, in the parable, Jesus turns the tables on the rich man, who in his torment needs help from Lazarus. The judgment is severe: As the rich man showed no mercy, he receives none.

Good Solutions That Miss the Mark

Liberation theologians are not only aware of the suffering among a large portion of the population; they are frustrated and angry about it.

Much of their frustration apparently stems from society's wrong diagnoses of the roots of the suffering, with the result that well-intended efforts and expenditures miss the target. Is the fundamental cause of poverty and oppression, as some "experts" proclaim, backward agricultural technology? Illiteracy? A failure to control population growth? Lack of industrialization? The absence of majority rule? A labor force deficient in discipline or in the "Protestant work ethic"?

To raise doubts about the primacy of these causes is not to question the worthiness of efforts to deal with them. Almost all such efforts are commendable and merit support. Nor is it to impugn the intentions of the champions of such efforts, whether they be in the World Bank, the Agency for International Development, the United Nations, the Inter-American Development Bank, or in numerous religious and charitable missions and foundations. Yet the proponents should take seriously the widespread perception in the Third World itself that few current "solutions" strike at the core of the problems.

When "uplift" programs imply that poor individuals substantially control their destiny and could, if they only would, solve their own difficulties, this further frustrates the oppressed. The very measures of progress associated with some "cures" are largely dependent on perspectives that gloss over social inequities. A rising Gross National Product in a Third World nation, for example, suggests a greater availability of consumer goods. From the bottom up, however, GNP progress is often seen as something achieved at the cost of social polarization, with the rich getting richer, the poor getting poorer. Also, a poor nation's statistically greater capital may be siphoned off so that the poor benefit little, if at all. This capital is swept from the country in various forms — as profits of multinational corporations, as interest to foreigners who fund the national debt, or as savings stashed abroad by a poor country's own wealthy nationals.[5]

Anger follows frustration. People who find no solutions look for villains. Deane William Ferm writes that a "major cause of poverty and oppression in Latin America has been and remains the economic policies of the United States government and of multinational corporations."[6] Those who take issue with such statements risk being labeled as apologists unless they can produce a more credible explanation of social maladies and a more appealing strategy for correcting them.

Liberation theologians are typically dissatisfied with European and North American models for Third World institutions. Centuries-old land tenure systems and capitalism's insatiable drive to acquire raw materials, accepted by outsiders as inevitable, seem oppressive, even demonic, to the landless. Often attacked is the preoccupation with materialism that colors much of the North American and European view of ownership.[7] Franz Hinkelammert, for example, in *The Ideological Weapons of Death: A Theological Critique of Capitalism*, affirms that while life must be concerned with things, a life cannot be truly human if it ignores relations with other humans and with nature.[8]

Freedom Seekers Inspired by the Bible

The underprivileged and their champions found in religion verification of their own sense that justice is concerned with the *entire community*, not merely with individuals. In the Promised Land, the community is the genuine inheritor of the land although, to be sure, individuals must be allotted their fair portion. In the Wasteland, individuals rule; in the Promised Land, a community or "a people" takes effective possession. This emphasis on people-hood or community is essential to an understanding of the quest for liberation.

Land for the people is a dominant theme in two books by Marcelo de Barros Souza. In *A Bíblia e a luta pela terra* ("The Bible and the Battle for the Land"), Souza shows how the desire for land by the landless people of Brazil is a window which opens up some of the passages and stories in the

Bible.[9] For instance, the story of Abraham takes on all sorts of different connotations when seen through the eyes of the homeless masses. As one might expect, the emphasis falls on God's promise to give Abraham and his community some land, rather than on the promise to make him a great nation. Souza's other book, *Nossos pais nos contaram* ("Our Fathers Told Us"), is a running commentary on the Old Testament as seen through the eyes of peasants who seek relief from an oppressive system of land tenure.[10] In it, the settlement of Canaan becomes a sociopolitical upheaval by the peasantry within Canaan. The Hebrews are the rebellious serfs and workers at the bottom of Canaanite society who join fleeing slaves from Egypt to overthrow the established order. The Old Testament, then, from this perspective, is the story of a broad egalitarian revolution which in large part was oriented toward land reform.

These two books came out of Souza's experiences in the basic ecclesial communities. These BECs—astoundingly, tens of thousands of them in Brazil and elsewhere—are attempts by clergy and lay people to act out liberation theology in their daily lives.[11]

Souza's writings are neither a political theory explaining how the poor can take possession of the land nor an economic theory explaining how society could benefit from this massive reform. The books reflect the voices of the community in the Wasteland, crying for something better. These voices articulate a belief that God disapproves of Latin American land practices, and thus it is no wonder the Bible has taken on such great significance in the basic ecclesial communities.[12]

The great biblical drama of the Exodus from bondage and the long struggle to reach the Promised Land, which shapes the form and content of this entire book, has often spoken poignantly to the oppressed. Anyone familiar with the imagery of the Negro spirituals knows how this story kept hope alive among blacks in the United States during their long period of bondage: "One more river—and that's the river of Jordan—there's one more river to cross." "Joshua fit de battle of Jerico, an' de walls came tumblin' down." "Tell ol' Pharaoh to let my people go."

Church Views on Land Tenure

What land policy liberates? How should land be possessed? How can the community best benefit from land? Concern with the role of land is a dominant theme of the Bible—as it is of today's Church, especially in Latin America—and as it is likely to become in nations trying to throw off the yoke of dictatorial communism.

Charles Avila, a Filipino peasant organizer and liberationist scholar who spent much time underground during the Marcos tyranny, produced a compilation of and commentary on patristic writings on land ownership, from which we have drawn many of the following citations:[13]

Basil the Great "criticizes those who make *idia*, or private, what should actually be *koina*, or public—'designed for the common use of all.' "[14] He thought that "basically, all persons have an equal right to the land, just as they all have an equal right to the air they breathe."[15]

Ambrose of Milan, in his homily on Naboth's vineyard, minces no words in excoriating land monopolists: " 'Shall ye alone dwell upon the earth?' (Is. 5:8) . . . Why do you arrogate to yourselves, ye rich, exclusive right to the soil?"[16]

John Chrysostom thunders that God "left the earth free to all alike. Why, then, if it is common, have you so many acres of land, while your neighbor has not a portion of it? . . . Is this not an evil, that you alone should enjoy what is common?"[17] Even if present owners are not responsible for the unjust acquisitions of their forebears, unless arrangements are rectified to provide for equal right to use, "property is nothing but a continuing and fresh robbery."[18]

Augustine, too, "points out that all possess in common whatever nature offers. . . . But human-made things are not possessed in common. Here, the rule for the property one may keep is self-sufficiency."[19] "Ownership arrangements should be made with a view to the proper use of goods and should preclude license or abuse."[20]

Addressing the Church's concern for a just distribution of God's gifts, Thomas Aquinas thought the political authority should limit (or assign conventions to) the way real property could be purchased. The rights of property were to be respected but always with an eye toward the common good.[21]

Pius XII, marking the fiftieth anniversary of Leo XIII's seminal encyclical, *Rerum Novarum*, asserted in 1941 that the right to own property should in no wise obstruct the flow of "material goods created by God to meet the needs of all men,"[22] a sentiment reaffirmed by John XXIII in *Mater et Magistra*.[23]

Chapter and Verse

In the following chapters we deal specifically with how the Lord's earth can benefit all people. We neither deny the complexities of the problems nor hold any illusion that focusing on misuses of land will automatically usher in God's kingdom.

Relying, however, on evidence that economic systems need not be socially destructive, we advance solutions that seem workable in the Third World, where land problems are so clearly a central issue, and elsewhere, such as the United States and Western Europe, where the inequities engendered by land arrangements may be less obvious. The litmus test of proposals we put forward is consistency with biblical or Christian principles and with the ideals of maximum political and economic freedom.

We have deliberately refrained in this book from setting forth a thoroughgoing theory of theological anthropology or any other kind of detailed theological rationale for our position. To have gone more deeply into such topics (as one of us has done elsewhere[24]) would necessarily have introduced complexities that would bore many potential readers and points of doctrinal contention that would needlessly alienate others. One of us brings a more Calvinistic and the other a more Wesleyan perspective to the discussion, but it is developed from general Christian beliefs that we hold mutually.

Our approach owes a large debt to Henry George, the nineteenth-century North American political economist and social philosopher who tackled these very questions before most of his contemporaries even acknowledged the existence of a growing land problem.[25] The main thrust of his ideas now appears more relevant than ever. Whatever minor disagreements we may have with him, we are persuaded that the path he blazed leads in the direction of the Promised Land.

We intend to be a voice in an ongoing conversation — the Church's conversation about the ownership and tenure of land. Much of our discourse has a Latin American context, because liberation theology arose in Latin America and has its greatest following there. Without intending to denigrate black, feminist, or any of the other varieties of liberation theology, we address it in the form in which it is best known and has made the most impact. Latin American liberation theologians, our partners in dialogue, while raising questions of universal scope, have naturally focused most poignantly on Latin American oppression. But their concerns, if rightly understood, are those of all who long for the Promised Land.

We trust it will be clear we do not embark upon this dialogue with a superior attitude of "ugly Americans." If we often prescribe for other nations, it is because the acuteness of their land problems so clearly dramatizes the opportunities for wholesome change.

For example, between 1967 and 1985, the Brazilian government's Superintendency for the Development of Amazônia (SUDAM) opened 8.4 million hectares for new development in the Amazon.

> The most recent tally has 631 ranches, whose average size is 24,000 hectares, given the go-ahead by SUDAM. The biggest ones were Liquigas (678,000 hectares), Suia-Missu (560,000), Volkswagen A.G. (139,000), and the Armour-Swift/King Ranch (72,000). Most of these were Brazilian subsidiaries of multinational corporations. The income from their Amazonian projects was not repatriated abroad, to foreigners, but went instead to Brazilians in the South.[26]

These companies, for the most part, cleared the trees off the land. In one municipality alone, Xapuri, 25,000 acres were burned annually in the late 1970s, with the result that over 320,000 people who had lived there were displaced by 130 new landowners who had come to control title to the land.[27] The clearing proved to be a human and ecological disaster. Many of the displaced people are now not only homeless, but jobless, having migrated and been forced into city slums. Many of those who remained in Xapuri now earn subsistence wages. While a family of rubber tappers and nut gatherers earned approximately $1,300 a year, a family of farmers and ranchers makes less than $800 from the same land.[28] Meanwhile, the destruction of the Amazon is partly responsible for the global warming experienced in the 1980s, with accompanying droughts, widespread starvation, and epidemics of amoebic dysentery and typhoid fever.[29]

The relative diffusion of land ownership in the United States makes some results of land monopoly less keenly felt here. But if what we have to say has relevance in the Third World, the routes to justice are no less pertinent in our own milieu. In the United States, ownership of surface land and mineral resources is increasingly concentrated, suggesting that our own land tenure institutions are in need of much the same fundamental alteration.

Our insistence upon the centrality of the land problem will doubtless strike many readers as simplistic. One such reader who examined a draft of this book in manuscript is a distinguished Protestant theologian who is essentially in sympathy with our approach. But he feels that we fail sufficiently to appreciate the extent to which transnational corporations dominate global trade and undercut the ability of people to shape their own destinies, and the seriousness of the issue of overpopulation.

The explosive expansion of transnationals since World War II has, indeed, introduced complexities that did not significantly exist when Henry George set forth his forceful argument for unlimited free trade.[30] A recent study, however, suggests that in the 1970s this process entered a new phase in which transnationals were increasingly obliged to compete with one another, and in which host nations came to learn to use this circumstance to their advantage.[31] The author remarks that competition among transnationals is least likely to occur in the extractive industries (mining, forestry, and agriculture), which depend most directly upon control of land and natural resources.

> Large investments of plant and capital are required to exploit natural resources. Once these investments are made and titles to exploit natural resources are granted, it is very difficult for competing enterprises to enter the scene. Governments, therefore, are not able to rely on pressures of competition to counter the resources of corporations.[32]

So the land problem would seem to underlie perhaps not all, but at least many of the most resented and intractable instances of domination by transnationals.

The land problem has, of course, a malignant bearing on the population problem, too, inasmuch as restricted access to land compresses populations, reducing economic opportunity and stressing the environment. We contend that, on the whole, where poverty is attributed to overpopulation, closer examination will reveal that the real culprit is the fact that people are denied access to natural opportunity except on terms dictated by a privileged few. Yet we also believe that overpopulation is an independent issue of extreme gravity and urgency. We hold this view more on ecological than on strictly economic grounds. It is a view for which one of us has argued in print.[33] The fact that we do not address it in these pages should not be taken to imply that we underestimate its importance.

In short, we recognize that the land problem is not the *only* social problem, and that the solution to it that we propose will not solve *all* social problems. But we maintain that it is the most basic social problem, and that its solution would do more to lift the curse of poverty than would anything else.

Following is a kind of road map of the biblical journey to the Promised Land, and thus to the rest of this book.

Chapter 2 details some mechanisms used to keep people in bondage, as exemplified in colonial Latin America.

Chapter 3 charts the struggle for liberation, with a look at land reforms that fall short of their goals.

Chapter 4 examines religious or philosophical concepts that have condemned people to remain in the Wasteland.

Chapter 5 takes a hard, unromantic look at poverty and the poor.

Chapter 6 shows why Wasteland circumstances — exploitation and oppression — persist after political independence and despite the great push for economic development.

Chapter 7 addresses Marxism, which has been a potent force in liberation theology.

Chapter 8 deals with intellectual roadblocks that support the rich and powerful who block the King's Highway out of the Wasteland.

Chapter 9 finds practical guidelines for enlightened land policies — strategies for claiming the Promised Land — in the laws of Moses, and indicates how they are being adapted in our times.

Chapter 10 recapitulates how to reach the Promised Land, but not before warning of the pitfalls once it is attained.

The Appendix tells about Henry George, who spelled out what genuine land reform looks like for the modern world.

2

Egyptian Bondage
in the New World

Latin American Colonialism and Its Legacy

Just as the Hebrews in Egypt toiled beneath the yoke of Pharaoh and his taskmasters, so did the peoples of Latin America for centuries endure bondage to colonial rulers. And just as remnants of the slave mentality persisted among the Hebrews in the wilderness, so does the legacy of colonial attitudes and institutions persist in Latin America today.

A System Justifying Suffering

The image of the dying Christ, his body bent on the cross, eyes rolled up in sockets, meekly longing for heaven, is very common in the popular Catholicism of Latin America. Also common is the image of the Blessed Virgin as a sad woman, dressed in mourning, with a sword running through her body.

These dolorous figures speak of centuries of impotence under Spanish and other foreign masters. They perpetuate human bondage by spreading the myth that people should search for happiness by mortifying the flesh. This view would seem to be a gross distortion of redemptive suffering in the Christian tradition in that it confuses Jesus' suffering death, and the sacrifices entailed in following him, with the concept that God somehow wants people to suffer.[1]

Even today many practicing Roman Catholics approach carnival as a temporary relief from a reality of suffering—a reality that was present yesterday and will be here tomorrow, always. In this sense, carnival is escapism—for a few days. Then real life continues.

The Spanish and Portuguese empires also left their imprint in the implied claim that the Promised Land is something like a monarchy, that is, a place where aristocrats have more rights and privileges than ordinary people. The historical origins of this are clear. The Treaty of Tordesillas of 1494 divided the yet-to-be-discovered continent of South America between the kings of Portugal and Spain, without any concern for the rights of any native inhabitants.[2] And in the papal bull *Inter Caeteris*, Alexander VI made King Ferdinand and Queen Isabella "lords and masters" of the New World. The continent's treasure stores of gold and silver, and later coffee and beef, were thrown open—to an elite. The Indians, of course, were not in this category. As common people, they worked with the understanding that others had first claim on their labor. The Europeans seeking their fortunes in the New World either received grants or were attached to others who had such grants. How did this system work?

How the Colonial System Worked

The *encomienda* was the basic instrument used by the Spanish empire for settling Latin America. This was a grant of Indians to an *encomendero* who assumed the obligation, in principle, of Christianizing and civilizing them. For their part, the Indians were required to provide labor and tribute to Spain in exchange.

Although in theory the encomienda was not a grant of land, in practice many of the encomenderos were also granted *mercedes*, or legal titles to the very large tracts that gave rise to the later estates.[3]

> In effect, once the *encomienda* system had been abolished, it was the control of land that made it possible to continue extracting a surplus from the native population. . . . The ownership of land [in Latin America] became the basis of a system of social domination of the mass of the people by a small ethnically and culturally differentiated minority.[4]

Although the Church in many instances affirmed its intention to look after the Indians, it has also traditionally affirmed the rights of a small minority to most of the good land in Latin America. Moreover, it has supported this oligarchy by often substituting a purely transcendent hope for the Promised Land.[5] A survey of land tenure in Latin America unmistakably reveals how the gifts of nature were reserved for a chosen few.

Two types of large landed estates arose in the colonial period and still mark modern-day Latin America. One is the *hacienda*, a large estate employed in raising cattle and a diversity of crops which are used on the ranch itself or are sold in the local markets. The other is the plantation, a one-crop farm specializing in the cultivation of a single exportable product. Most of the plantations established in the sixteenth and seventeenth centuries were sugarcane plantations in northeast Brazil. They were managed by Europeans but worked by slaves usually brought over from Africa.[6]

Many of these large landholdings, especially the haciendas, originated as crown grants to important Spanish or Portuguese settlers. The European settlers were given not only the land, but also the labor of the Indians, who were initially their slaves. Later the "freed" Indians were tied to the landowners through debts brought on by a subsistence wage system. Both types of estates concentrated the land under a handful of select owners while exploiting the main body of the population. "The shortage of land off the estate, and its poor quality, enabled the landlord to attract or coerce labour into the estate without much difficulty."[7]

Rural and Urban Subjugation Persist

This pattern continues today with an underclass largely descended from the Indian and African slaves, along with other dispossessed groups. Yet the desperate faces one is apt to see in the slums of Rosario and Valparaiso or in the newly peopled jungles of Rondonia are not uniformly dark in hue. One also finds there many a fair-skinned visage of Teutonic or Slavic cast belonging to the child or grandchild of immigrants who came to Argentina, Chile, or Brazil seeking opportunity, only to be ultimately victimized by systems of privilege still harsher than those they had left behind.

Today's hacienda and plantation rely on cheap labor and are notorious for the hardships suffered by their tenants.[8] Two aspects of this oppressive pattern in Latin America should be emphasized. The first is that the hacienda and the plantation generally produce fewer benefits for the local populace than do the family farms of Europe and North America. The second is that the system of exploitation, far from being confined to the rural sector, pervades the urban and industrial sectors as well.

The hacienda is especially noted for its inefficient husbandry. In part, these large estates are not very productive because the landowners face few social or economic pressures to become good farm managers. Social prestige in Latin America is attached to *owning* land, rather than to using land efficiently. The hacienda is thus more a source of security and power than a business. Oftentimes, the owners live in the city where they pursue social or professional interests while leaving the running of the estates to overseers. Consequently, the landowners often do not make a large profit; but then, that is not their objective. Labor is cheap, and the cost of holding on to huge estates—in other words, the taxes charged by the public for the privilege of retaining possession—are low or effectively nonexistent. Strong incentives for good stewardship of the land are absent to owners of both the hacienda and the plantation.[9]

Meanwhile, most of the populace is excluded from the fruits of the land. The laborers do not share in the profits of the hacienda. The contrast between the grand plantation house and the miserable workers' huts is as striking in Latin America as it was in the antebellum South of the United States. Most crops grown chiefly for export, such as sugar and coffee, provide inadequate nourishment for the people, and the poor seldom eat the beef raised on the haciendas. Land that might be used for growing rice and beans is given over to raising export crops.

It has been argued that raising export crops represents the optimum market use of much land. But tenures are disposed in such a way that the general population partakes meagerly, at most, in proceeds that could otherwise make rice and beans for them a diet of volition rather than of necessity. Further, acreage best suited for the cultivation of rice and beans often is not employed at all.

This situation is exacerbated by the huge national debt of countries such as Brazil and Mexico. Government policy then becomes oriented toward reducing the balance of payments at the expense of staple goods.[10]

Moreover, this colonial system of land tenure discourages the creation of capital. There are several types of workers on the haciendas and plantations. The haciendas in the Andean highlands have traditionally relied on Indian workers who have exchanged their labor for the right to farm small plots of land. The haciendas (or *fazendas*, as they are called in Portuguese) and the plantations in southern Brazil have usually been worked by landless day laborers who are hired during the sowing and harvest seasons. In northeast Brazil, the workers have been tied to the estates through debts to the landlord. In any event, the workers have been paid minimal wages, providing subsistence, but certainly no surplus for investment.

The landowners, of course, gain a surplus, notoriously high in some cases, but often less than is frequently assumed. The safety net for landlords is the land itself. What hurts the Latin nations and their people is that the surplus from the land is often spent on luxury goods that are either imported, thereby straining the country's balance of payments, or are produced in Latin America at the expense of other more useful manufacture.[11] Meanwhile, the giant agribusinesses do accumulate profits but send most of them out of Latin America for reinvestment in the United States and Europe.[12]

What about the nonrural aspect of this pattern of the Wasteland? Latin American exploitation through land monopoly also creates an extreme urban class division between the very poor worker and the very rich owner. The latter, although typically nonproductive himself, controls the means of production and dominates the sociopolitical system.

Some of the worst examples of colonial abuse in Latin America occurred in the mining industry. In Colombia it was the gold, silver, and emerald mines—not the plantations—that fueled the early economy of the colony. These mines were worked first by Indians, sometimes brought in from great distances, and later by black slaves. Land grants such as the mercedes were actually surface grants. The Crown retained all subsoil mineral rights and for the most part leased the mines on a percentage agreement. The Indian laborers were drafted to their work, which was seen as a form of tax payment.[13]

The mining resources, like the agricultural resources, were alienated from Indian groups and gradually concentrated in fewer and fewer hands. The mines financed the administration of the colony, enriched the royal family, and attracted many settlers who came from Spain to seek their fortune. In Colombia, land use for agriculture actually followed the lead of the mining industry. Small-plot subsistence cultivation developed adjacent to the mining areas, and mine operators established a cattle industry to provide protein and a sugarcane industry to provide liquor for the slave gangs.[14]

As cities and commerce developed, the power of the wealthy carried over to urban areas. Industrial workers, like their rural counterparts, work for extremely low wages. Landless country people, frequently evicted from the haciendas and plantations, are drawn to the cities through word of mouth, radio, television, and movies that present the cities as if they were the Promised Land. This picture, of course, is false. Because there are so many landless folk seeking employment, the cities also are places of great degradation. Urban land monopoly and speculation create tremendous housing difficulties for the poor. For example, according to data provided by John Garrison, Area Representative for Brazil of the Inter-American Foundation, whereas in 1950, 36% of Brazil's population lived in cities, by 1988, 75% lived in cities. Thus, the population of the city of São Paulo, Brazil, has grown from ca. 2.2 million in 1950 to ca. 17 million today. It is little wonder, then that on a 1989 trip to São Paulo, one of the authors was informed that more than one-third of the city's inhabitants were *favelados* (that is, landless urban squatters) and that over 2.5 million were street children. They are crowded into slums and shantytowns — the urban Wasteland.

According to Andre Gunder Frank:

> The monopolization of land and other resources necessarily results in the exploitation of the nonmonopolized resources, that is, labor, and in the underutilization of all resources. Thus, one primary purpose of the ownership of large amounts of land, both on the individual and on the social level, is not to use it but to prevent its use by others. These others, denied access to the primary resource, necessarily fall under the domination of the few who do control it. And then they are exploited in all conceivable ways, typically through low wages.[15]

For the most part, the first European settlements in Latin America arose as administrative centers. Their economic purpose was twofold: to facilitate the collection of taxes and to organize Indian labor. One must look back with shame to realize that Christian baptism was often used as a tool to supplant the natives' worldview with one which facilitated their subjugation.

Typically, these early towns were situated in areas of concentrated

Indian populations. Lima, Quito, and Cuzco are examples. Since the economy of South America was oriented to Europe, these early centers were also often paired with port settlements such as Callao, the outport of Lima. Many of the early towns were mining towns, but whether based on administration and tax collection or on mining, the formative principle of these early towns was the same as that of the plantation: They facilitated an elitist rule of a region and the removal of natural resources and crops for shipment overseas. From the beginning, the economy of the cities, like that of the estates, was founded on human exploitation.

One Continent's Example of a World in Bondage

Obviously, this impoverishment of the majority of the inhabitants to support the enrichment of a small group is in no way confined to Latin America. Virtually every nation — even those considered most advanced, such as the United States — has very poor people who are abused by systems that allow too much wealth and power to rest in the hands of too few.

The focus here is on Latin America for two reasons. First, it gave birth to the liberation theology movement that is trying to come to grips with these problems. Second, its history and present institutions dramatically illustrate how many of the socioeconomic problems of our age originated with the belief that the land and its fruits belong only to a select few.

By denying or ignoring any rights of native peoples to "their" land, the Treaty of Tordesillas set a pattern of mineral and crop exploitation, beginning with gold and silver and cacao and continuing with copper, tin, nitrates, hardwoods, rubber, petroleum, bananas, sugar, and coffee. The natural resources and the bounty of the land have been removed and sent to Europe and North America at great profit, but with little benefit to most Latin Americans.

As mentioned, the haciendas, plantations, and mines concentrated power in the hands of the landowners. The system of land tenure actually made the laborers not only subservient to, but almost completely dependent on, the owners; so, all too generally, do they even now remain.

3

Perceptions of the Promised Land

Struggles for Liberation

Notwithstanding the once-popular image of happy, carefree peasants on the one hand, and despite the persistence of fatalistic and escapist postures on the other, it is now understood that, by and large, the underclasses envision something better for themselves and their children. As a consequence, many Latin American countries have attempted to institute some type of land reform.

The Promise of Land Reform

Since the structures of oppression were not developed autonomously, many of the reforms were aimed at foreign exploitation. Examples of these are the nationalization of the oil fields in Chile in 1923, in Argentina in 1924, in Mexico in 1938, in Brazil in 1950, and in Peru in 1969.[1] Sometimes, however, the expropriation has targeted advantaged groups within their own countries. This occurred with the nationalization of Bolivia's tin industry in 1952, when more than half of the industry was owned by the Patino family.[2] Interestingly, following the colonial practice of reserving gold and silver for the king, it is more characteristic in Latin America than in England or the United States to legislate public ownership or control over subsurface mineral resources.

Despite this tendency to legislate control over mines, oil, and gas, Latin American governments have made relatively few real attempts at rural land reform and virtually none at urban land reform.

One of the better-known attempts at agrarian reform occurred in Mexico. After expropriation of the Church's estates in the mid-1800s,[3] the distribution of land in Mexico became so concentrated that it is commonly claimed that 1 percent of the population owned 97 percent of the land and

96 percent of the population owned 1 percent of the land.[4] By 1910, .02 percent of the agricultural population were estate owners, 88.4 percent were landless laborers. All this helps explain why Mexico's revolution came in 1911.

The goal of the new Mexican constitution of 1917 was to redistribute some of the land among the peasants, directly in small holdings, and as grants called *ejidos* to communities. The latter allowed individuals the right to cultivate plots of community land without buying or renting them. The idea of the ejido seemed good, because there was not enough land to give small holdings to all the landless laborers.

The redistribution scheme reached a large number of people. Government figures indicate that over a quarter of the national territory (more than 55 million hectares) was expropriated and redivided between 1924–1970. And yet the ejidos have not proven successful.[5] They flourished as long as the state propped them up with credit, water resources, transportation and marketing advantages, and technical assistance. When this special support was withdrawn, they could no longer compete with private farms.

Bolivia's agrarian reform occurred in 1953, approximately a year after the revolution that brought Victor Paz Estenssoro to the presidency for the first time.[6] When this took place, 95 percent of the farmland was held by 8 percent of the landowners in holdings of 500 or more hectares. Most often, workers on these large estates had permission to graze a few head of livestock and to cultivate a small plot of land for themselves in lieu of wages. That is, most of the agricultural population worked under a share-cropping or peonage system. Article 12 of the 1953 agrarian reform law attacked this semifeudal system by abolishing some of the large estates called *latifundios*, which were labor intensive and utilized archaic forms of agriculture. Those large estates that utilized modern farming methods and some medium-sized estates were also expropriated in part, and the land given to unsalaried tenants. Between 1953–1970, the government redistributed 11.7 million hectares of land to 266,066 families.

Sven Lindqvist observes that "it is in Bolivia that the land reform has been toughest."[7] There, unlike the other agrarian reform countries of South America, there has been, as a rule, no compensation to the landlords. Despite all this, the *finqueros*, or big estate owners, managed to retain one-fifth of the arable soil and more than half the grazing areas.[8]

In Peru, land reform occurred when General Velasco Alvarado usurped power in 1968.[9] The Velasco government quickly expropriated the cattle and farmlands of Cerro de Pasco, a corporation based in the United States, and in 1969 passed a law legalizing the expropriation of all large estates tied to foreign control of agricultural exports. One of the goals of the legislation was to allow the state to take control of the sugar industry. The original intention of the law was not to divide the estates into small land-holdings but rather to reorganize them into state-supported cooperative or collective units. Between 1969 and 1976, the reform affected over one-third of the rural population and almost one-half of the farmland of Peru. Stocks in industry were given in compensation to farmers whose lands were expropriated. The nationalist reforms in Peru, however, are generally regarded as ineffectual in achieving their major goals.[10]

Peru, although much more liberal in compensating its multinationals, had actually followed the Cuban model in the attempt to free its agriculture from foreign domination. Before Castro's revolution, thirteen North American sugar companies held over 1.2 million hectares of land in Cuba.[11] Under the agrarian reform laws of 1959, Cuba expropriated these and other properties occupied by foreigners. Castro replaced the large landholding companies with cooperatives and state farms. Also, all estates larger than 402 hectares were expropriated in 1959, with some compensation, and the lands distributed in 27-hectare plots to the tenants. In this way over 100,000 peasants became landowners. Later, the maximum number of hectares permitted for private holdings was reduced from 402 to 67 hectares, the state then expropriating an additional 1.8 million hectares. Although some of this land was redistributed among landless peasants, the tendency since 1963 has been to transfer land ownership to the state while guaranteeing the workers a specified wage plus other benefits. The cooperatives that did not successfully manage their sugar estates, for example, were abolished in favor of state-directed systems.

Failures of Land Reform

Have these examples of rural land redistribution programs and nationalization materially eliminated oppression in Latin America? Unfortunately, effective land reform in Latin America, as elsewhere, has scarcely taken place. To cite this failure is not to minimize the serious barriers to success that have frustrated attempts to institute wholesome land policies in the Third World.

One of the major obstacles is that many governments are run or controlled by a powerful elite that owns the most valuable land. Oftentimes the implementation of reform legislation is blocked by these landowners, who retard and corrupt the process. Foreign enterprises also fight the reforms; when they threaten to withdraw their investments, their arguments carry great weight. They are aided by fiscally conservative politicians who argue that maintaining stability, even if it means closing one's eyes to the oppression of the poor, is necessary for economic development.

Meanwhile, those who stand to benefit—the miners and rural workers— tend to be poorly represented. When they are illiterate as well as economically deprived, their ability to exert pressure for change seems almost hopelessly handicapped, no match for the power structures arrayed against them. Where thoroughgoing expropriation has occurred, as in Cuba, the result has been a degree of collectivist regimentation that destroys initiative and exchanges private oppression for state oppression—surely a cruel counterfeit and betrayal of the authentic vision of liberation.

In Bolivia, the land program itself, despite its flaws, could likely have made possible for most people at least a modicum of material self-sufficiency. Unfortunately, it was accompanied and followed by other programs that wrecked the entire economy and plunged a vast majority of the population into a state of destitution, if anything, more pathetic than before. The nationalization of large segments of commerce and industry undercut motives for productive initiative and exertion. Unrealistic benefit measures (demanded by the powerful Marxist-oriented miners' unions) did the same, while pricing Bolivian tin and other metals out of the world market. This sprawling edifice of welfare and bureaucracy rested upon a base of public debt so unsustainable that by July 20, 1985, the value of the Bolivian peso had fallen to the point where, at the desk of the La Paz Sheraton, the wife of one of the authors exchanged a single United States dollar for 850,000 pesos! Less than a month later, the structure's principal architect, Paz Estenssoro, was returned to power and, to his credit, proceeded to dismantle it. But the land reform, for which he had also been largely responsible, remains essentially in place.

Latin America's most promising approach to land reform was the "Law of Emphyteusis" adopted in 1826 under the influence of Argentina's founding president, Bernardino Rivadavia.[12] Its enactment brought immediate results in new settlements, new employment opportunities, and the cultivation of hitherto neglected lands. A series of decrees was promulgated to correct administrative defects, but before they became operative, Rivadavia resigned. His bitter opponent, Colonel Dorrengo, proceeded to emasculate the program, a process completed by dictator Juan Manuel de Rosas. Then Rosas conferred huge land grants upon himself and his minions, eliminating almost wholly the public collection of ground rent. The inland provinces became practically depopulated. The Emphyteutic Law, by then a mere cipher, was finally repealed in 1857, and "the domination of the country by a landowning oligarchy was consolidated."[13]

"Land reform" as a political slogan is used at times to imply redistribution, at times increased productivity, but those using the term seem purposefully to leave it vague and without real pin-down meaning. In general usage it refers almost exclusively to rural rather than to industrial or urban programs. On the whole, Latin American governments have found it easier to target foreign holdings, such as the Grace sugar properties in Peru, than to target their own nationals who actually hold most of the large estates.

The few land reforms that were implemented have been plagued by a host of problems. Some legislation perversely led landowners to evict tenants, replacing them with tractors and day laborers. Distributive laws often created a multiplicity of small, uneconomic holdings whose owners lacked expertise, money for machinery, and the means to bring their produce to markets. In other cases, new landowners were at the mercy of businessmen who exploited them. The present upper class, in fact, in the aftermath of "reform," seems to be based on the monopolistic control of commerce, distribution, and regional political power. Former landowners, after being compensated for their expropriated holdings, became traders and money-lenders, positioning themselves to continue their exploitation as before. Without a base in land, however, their power could scarcely be sustained indefinitely in the absence of the political favoritism they now enjoy.

In *Land and Power in South America*, Lindqvist presents a compelling exposition of the cardinal role that land monopoly has played in the anguish of that unhappy continent, and of the pathetic inadequacy of such reform as has been attempted. When it comes to prescribing alternatives, however, he offers the communes of mainland China as a model—one, we might add, that has since been largely abandoned there as economically ineffi-cient.[14]

Envisioning the Promised Land

Turning to their religious heritage for answers to the severe injustice and suffering stemming from concentrated land ownership seems natural enough to liberation theologians and their followers.

What of that large body of modern intellectuals and their followers who write and act as if God is irrelevant, if not dead? Can they bring themselves to take a hard look at the old truths behind the biblical stories to see if they might shed new light on today's renewed search for freedom and justice? One hopes they will not close their minds to potent and challenging interpretations of economics and social ethics because they happen to be found in the Old and New Testaments.

If those of us in the Wasteland of the twentieth century have trouble visualizing the Promised Land, this is not a novel phenomenon. We are similar to the people of the Exodus in this respect. They kept thinking of what they were leaving behind, weeping over the lost fish, cucumbers, mel-ons, and onions of Egypt (Num. 11:5). Moses and the people had heard of the land of their forefathers and had dreamed of it in Egypt and in the wilderness, but they couldn't quite imagine it or trust in it. Thus, as they approached Canaan, they sent spies to see if the land was in fact good or bad, rich or poor (Num. 13:17–20).

The spies brought back visible evidence: figs and pomegranates and a single cluster of grapes so heavy that two men had to carry it between them on a pole. So the land was good.

False Reports and Their Consequences

According to the Old Testament story, however, the spies also brought back a false report: "The land," they said, "devours its inhabitants" (Num.

13:32). This false report ultimately prevented the people of that generation from leaving the Wasteland. They were so frightened by the report that they sought a captain to lead them back to Egypt. Because they refused to trust in what God had promised, they were excluded from the land and doomed to live out their lives in the Wasteland.

We today, like the Hebrew wanderers, are victimized by disinformation concerning the Promised Land. For instance, we are often told that the Promised Land is purely otherworldly or spiritual. In this context, it is not a land where men and women get their hands dirty planting corn, working a lathe, or handling money. Rather, it is more like a cathedral, a refuge, a place to be comforted while enduring empty bellies or dying children. When this is the message organized religion conveys, it is no wonder so many have turned their backs upon it.

According to this false report, politics and social reform offer no real solutions to the problems humanity faces. Overt interest in the land approaches sin, because man's focus should be on what is eternal rather than on what is temporal. Commitment to land reform is, from this perspective, thought of as more a temptation than a virtue.

This image of a Promised Land that is only spiritual seems very prevalent in Latin America. Under the influence of North American pietism, Latin American Pentecostals have sometimes so strongly emphasized the transcendence of Christ that his message of the reign of righteousness has been utterly erased. These Christians see themselves, in the imagery of First Peter, as exiles whose true home is in heaven; they are merely passing through this world on their way to the next, trying not to get too involved with the grubby aspects of the trip. Brazilian Protestants don't dance at carnival; they go on retreats.[15] Catholics, as we have said, may dance, but only as a brief escape.

In Umbanda and other Afro-Christian cults, the retreat from the material world is even more complete. These spiritists claim that the material world is something of an illusion. Therefore, many of the promises of the *orixas*, or minor gods, lead the adherents to focus on trying to control hidden forces and to neglect the issues concerning daily work on the land.[16]

The notion that the Promised Land is "spiritual only" is often coupled with the claim that God intends the material world to be a place of suffering. To the extent this keeps people from admitting the very possibility of overcoming physical oppression, it plays into the hands of their oppressors and helps to perpetuate social inequities.

Consider the implications when Christians and others sharply distinguish the things of the flesh, which are deemed to be bad or unworthy of attention, from the things of the spirit, which are seen to be so all-important they crowd out all else. Those accepting this perspective tend to hand all things material over to evil. The world to them becomes a place of testing where they are called upon to withstand all manner of burdens heaped upon them. Instead of revolting against suffering, they glory in it.

Who Owns the Promised Land?

This discussion of the meaning of life is not far removed, as one might at first suspect, from the incomplete attempts at land reform discussed earlier.

There exists a parallel between these ineffectual reforms and the Israelites' half-hearted attempt to enter the Promised Land. The Israelites lost their resolve and their faith. Instead they believed "the slander upon the land," brought back by the spies (Num. 14:36). In the modern world, and Latin America in particular, the slander is twofold: There is the false claim that for all but an exalted few the Promised Land is exclusively other-worldly—a hope without real-world substance. The second part of the slander is that the land and its fruits belong to the few people who claim to own them, rather than to the entire community of God's children.

It is instructive to consider why the Israelites began to doubt God's promises concerning the land. Having seen the wondrous fruit, they thought the land must belong to giants—while they themselves seemed like mere grasshoppers (Num. 13:33). They saw the land as belonging to the sons of Anak, powerful by birth. Rather than questioning their perception of who owned the land, they questioned God's sovereignty. They were more willing to banish God's promises from history into mythology than they were to doubt the false reports. They trembled before the aristocracy of Canaan and were even ready to return to Egypt. They convinced themselves that the Canaanite giants were the true owners of the land and forgot that the earth is the Lord's. That was their sin that occasioned God's anger and their punishment—exile to the Wasteland.

In the Bible, the Promised Land is characterized by the "eminent domain" of God. Thus, after the forty years in the Wasteland, when a new generation finally entered into the land across the Jordan, Joshua reminded the people of how *the Lord* had given them the land with the fruit of the vineyards and olive groves, and he then made a covenant before them with God, saying, "as for me and my house, we will serve the Lord" (Josh. 24:13–15).

Was this eminent domain just a device for giving the Israelites a home? Or does God's will for the land not have a deeper significance for all humanity in all times and all places? In the New Testament, the category of the Promised Land is completely subsumed under the more comprehensive rubric of "the reign [or kingdom] of God."[17] Take, for example, Jesus' instructions about seeking food and clothing in Luke 12:22–31 and Matthew 6:25–33. His tone is sarcastic as he pokes fun at the disciples for being anxious about those things. This sarcasm does not reflect a belief that food and clothes are unimportant, as if the spiritual world calls for the abnegation of warmth and a satisfied belly. To the contrary, he affirms that "all the nations of the world seek these things; and your Father knows that you need them" (Luke 12:30; Matt. 6:32). Jesus' sarcasm is directed at the foolish notion that these things, which all people need and want, can come in harmonious plenitude outside of the structures of God's reign (Luke 12:31; Matt. 6:33).

The abundance of the land comes only with the recognition that the earth is the Lord's. Otherwise, we continue in the Wasteland.

When Jesus said, "Blessed are you poor, for yours is the kingdom of God" (Luke 6:20; cf. Matt. 5:3), he was affirming the justice of God's reign. Jesus was saying that the poor can be of good comfort in God's kingdom, because there they will not be exploited.

Note that Jesus held to a prophetic view of what caused poverty. For the prophets, poverty was the consequence of human exploitation. Nowhere is this clearer than with Amos, who called forth destruction upon Israel:

> because they sell the righteous for silver,
>   and the needy for a pair of shoes—
> they that trample the head of the poor into the dust of the earth
>   and turn aside the way of the afflicted (Amos 2:6–7).

Jesus was simply affirming this view of poverty when he paired the beatitudes with woes in Luke 6:20-26. Jesus cursed the rich because Jesus, like Amos, perceived the connection between the rich men's wealth and the misery of other people.

For Jesus, like Amos and the other prophets, righteousness entails a right relationship among persons, and right acting leads to well-being. Jeremiah thought that if the people would "execute justice one with another," then God would let them dwell in the land that he gave of old to the fathers forever (Jer. 7:5–7). Justice, it cannot be stressed too much, is the essential mark of the Promised Land.

The biblical meanings of justice are many, but what are the characteristics of doing justice that pertain directly to the ownership and use of land? To do justice means to perceive and be responsible to the needs of the community as a whole, as Paul pointed out to the Corinthian Christians. He reminded them that God's righteousness consists of scattering his abundance abroad, giving to the poor (2 Cor. 9:9–10), and making God's bounty (natural opportunity) available to all.

This helps explain why the early Church held possessions in common. Those who possessed property felt responsible for those in need. Thus, "there was not a needy person among them, for as many as were possessors of lands or houses sold them, and brought the proceeds of what was sold and laid it at the apostles' feet; and distribution was made to each as any had need" (Acts 4:34–35). There was no room for accumulating an excess or for holding land unproductive and hoarding it as a personal reserve of wealth. As Ananias and Sapphira found out, to hold back the proceeds of the land from the community was to cheat God (Acts 5:3).

This particular aspect of justice harks back to the Mosaic laws concerning land tenure, based on the proposition that the land belongs to God.[18] Thus, land could not be sold in perpetuity. It could not be treated as an absolute possession by the Israelites, who were simply visitors in his land (Lev. 25:23). While God was considered a gracious host who intended the land to yield fruit and to be a place of security for all, his ownership was to be respected by keeping the ordinances that he established over the land (Lev. 25:18–19). Because one of the purposes of these land laws was to help extend God's benevolence to everyone, a farm was not to be stripped bare during the harvest; gleanings and fallen grapes were to be left for the poor and the sojourner (Lev. 19:9–10; 23:22). This statute was blunt: To disobey was to steal (Lev. 19:11–13).

Landlordism versus Righteousness

A leap from Old Testament days to modern times reminds us that these justice and land-tenure issues persist throughout history.

In these remarkable 1990s, people who are throwing off the yoke of communism in pursuit of the advantages of free markets are nevertheless wary about accepting the excesses and disparities of capitalism. Whether they realize it or not, they are seeking to partake in the ancient divine promise. For while the Promised Land offers individuals opportunities for private gain, it does so only within the framework of opportunities for the community as a whole to live and work under God's reign—that is, under right relations with the land and with each other.

Is not this perception of what human life on earth should be at the core of Christian tradition? In his encyclical *Quadragesimo Anno*, for instance, Pius XI explains the intent of Leo XIII's words, "The earth even though apportioned among private owners, ceases not thereby to minister to the needs of all" (*Rerum Novarum*, art. 4) in the following way:

> Now, not every kind of distribution of wealth and property among men is such that it can satisfactorily, still less adequately, attain the end intended by God. Wealth therefore, which is constantly being augmented by social and economic progress, must be so distributed among the individuals and classes of society that the common good of all, of which Leo XIII spoke, be thereby promoted. In other words, the good of the whole community must be safeguarded.
>
> Each class, then, must receive its due share, and the distribution of created goods must be brought into conformity with the demands of the common good and social justice. For every sincere observer realizes that the vast differences between the few who hold excessive wealth and the many who live in destitution constitute a grave evil in modern society.[19]

Again, the danger of confining our vision of the Promised Land to a nebulous fantasy is particularly present in our age. The attempt to separate church and state, when it has not eliminated God altogether, tends to imprison him in a spiritual realm divorced from such earthy topics as land tenure. Instead of a history propelled by the ideal of the good society — God's social order, one might say — people have let the march of events be guided to a great extent by private and collective selfishness, pride, and power hunger. Even those who claim a religious orientation often seem to have restricted God's role to the influence he exerts exclusively on individuals, assuming society can then take care of itself. This, of course, avoids facing up to those beliefs and actions that deny the bounty of the Lord's earth to all humankind. While carrying this restricted and distorted picture of the Promised Land, people still naïvely hope that individuals will somehow act decently one to another.[20]

To correct this narrow view of the Promised Land and to achieve its liberating potential, as the adherents of liberation theology have been trying to do, is to acknowledge God's sovereignty over the land and to take seriously Jesus' petition, "Thy will be done, on earth as it is in heaven." As long as we convince ourselves to the contrary that the land really belongs to a privileged group of people who claim to own it and that the earth's fruits were intended almost exclusively for their benefit, we will remain in the Wasteland.

Moses led his people out of slavery, yet, in the end, he presents a somewhat tragic figure. After spending his life in the hope of reaching the Promised Land, he was excluded from it. Our last picture of Moses, before he dies in Moab, finds him on Pisgah looking down across the Jordan, seeing — but not being able to enter — the place that he had struggled for so long to reach.

In part, Moses' exclusion, as already noted, was the consequence of the "evil report of the land" (Num. 14). But the full reason he was barred from the land relates to his own response to the doubts about God's promise. Moses, as leader of the community, was held responsible for its lack of faith (Num. 14:11, 26–38). God's accusation to Moses was: "You did not believe in me, to sanctify me in the eyes of the people of Israel" (Num. 20:12).

Rooted in this accusation is a relevant question that presses upon civilization at the brink of the twenty-first century, a question that speaks to the rights of all people to land in Latin America and virtually every continent: Do we really believe that the earth is the Lord's? If so, how are we responsible for making this a sacred principle — for sanctifying God — in the eyes of the people?

It is painfully obvious that most land laws in today's world have little affinity with the biblical view that the land has been provided for the benefit of all. Unfortunately, most Christians, along with adherents of other religions, lend tacit approval to these laws that effectively deprive most people of their birthrights to the land. In that, we stand with both feet planted in the Wasteland — or, at best, like Moses on the mountain, seeing the distant Promised Land but unable to dwell there.

Is it not our responsibility to turn this vision into something more than a hope? How can one help our generation leave the Wasteland? A closer look at the philosophical underpinnings that keep us in the Wasteland is perhaps a necessary first step. To this topic we now turn.

4

Viewing Life from the Wasteland

The Righteous Society versus Baal Worship

Sharply disparate views of the role of politics created tensions and exasperation in the Latin American Church in the first half of this century, providing fertile ground for the emergence of liberation theology.

One problem encountered was how to acknowledge God's sovereignty in history when the everyday world was structured in ways that seemed to deny it. Where could one look for a divine presence in a civilization that, in many ways, seemed so uncivilized? And was it up to individuals or government to establish a reign of righteousness?

Church and Government — Models from the Past

Of the many answers to this set of questions that have come down the ages, Leonardo Boff points to three historical models of the Church that have particularly impacted the liberation dialogue in Latin America. The first, which he calls "The Church as City of God," holds that politics and government should be considered to be essentially outside the realm of religion. They serve their function of binding society together while individuals, one by one, find salvation. The second, which he calls "The Church as *Mater et Magistra*," holds that the Church should try to educate and persuade the political leaders, so that they, imbued with the Christian spirit, may work for the social betterment of all. The third model, which Boff calls "The Church as Sacrament of Salvation," holds that the religious community should open itself to the world and actively collaborate with the state as it plays its role in uplifting the members of society.[1]

Boff is of the opinion that the first of these models is not nearly as influential today as during colonial times. It still exists, however. In a sense, "The Church as City of God" is the Latin American Roman Catholic position developed as a distortion of Augustine's reappraisal of the Roman Empire after the sack of Rome in 410. Although Augustine was convinced that the political organization of society was not natural to man, he nevertheless considered it essential.[2] Politics, as he saw it, attempts to counteract the social disorder resulting from man's sinful condition. Given man's fallen state, government, while admittedly oppressive, is necessary and even useful. The state, recognizing that the ultimate destiny and welfare of people lie outside its boundaries, should establish conditions that simply allow people to pursue God. According to Augustine, the state certainly could not actively promote salvation through legislation and coercion. At best, perhaps, secular society could establish conditions that allowed people to pursue their own salvation in relative peace.

Augustine thought that eternal categories such as "sin" and "salvation" do not apply to the state as an entity, but to individuals, good and bad, upright and perverse, joined in one common society. The seeds of the end-time community are already present, but the separation between those predestined to eternal glory and those predestined to eternal torment will become visible only with the final judgment. Until then, the state attempts to provide order, temporal peace, and security to society as a whole — to both the wicked and the righteous.

As practiced in Latin America, Boff describes the Church as City of God as a

> Church that is almost exclusively turned in on itself. ... The world has no theological value for this Church; it must be converted because only through the mediation of the Church can it arrive at the state of grace (*ordo gratiae*). Because its field of activity is strictly bound to the sacred, the Church is found to be insensitive to human problems that arise beyond its borders, in the world and in society. The political realm is "tarnished" and is to be avoided at all costs. More than neutral, the Church is indifferent to "worldly" realities.[3]

The position that political activity should be an engine of social betterment traces its roots in Latin America not to Augustine, but to the ferment of the creole movement for independence and to ideas generated by Dom Pedro II, who, as Brazil's last monarch, freed the slaves there in 1888.[4] With regard to the function of the Church in secular society, this view reflects both the Church as Mater et Magistra and the Church as Sacrament of Salvation.

According to Boff, the Church carried on its missionary activity in colonial Latin America within the constraints of a pact that it had made with the plutocracy. After the birth of the new independent nations, the Church adjusted its agreement in the following way: It approached the upper classes, who had the power to help the poor, and tried to educate and persuade them to do so. A pact of mutual benefit was formed by the civil and religious authorities, and as a consequence, Latin American governments established many programs of social relief and human assistance. To use Boff's characterization, the Church became a Church *for* the poor. It emerged as Mother and Teacher.

This model of the Church is itself authoritarian and is comfortable with authoritarian regimes. It tries not to interfere directly with civil rule, preferring to exert a quiet influence by evangelizing and converting the governing elite. But, according to Boff, this "model of the Church is often too committed to secular powers to assume a critical stance toward the oppression that embitters the life of the poor."[5]

Like the first two, Boff's third historical model of the Church in Latin America is, in his opinion, too passive in its stance against existing oppressive social structures. This third model is the one embraced by most modern-day Christians and by the Second Vatican Council. It affirms modernization and trusts in "progress" and "development."

According to this model, humans are thought to be social by nature. However, what unites people is not, as Augustine maintained, that they hunger for God, but that their minds are capable of thinking God's thoughts after him. Humankind is endowed with reason and, in turn, reason—both discursive and intuitive—provides the best clues to the will of God. Thus the minds of people should be kept open to truth; no questions or sources of truth should be closed.

In Boff's words:

> The Church opened itself to the world. The principal problems were . . . linked to society: justice, social participation, and integral development for everyone. In this way the Church . . . came to value science and the relative worth of earthly realities, developing an ethics of progress and thereby committing itself to social transformation, participating in all the great debates concerning education, economic development, unions, and agrarian reform.[6]

Here, people almost become partners with God as they help build a better world. Evil, which comes from the absence of reason, is conquered through education, free elections, open discourse, and the like. The state (individuals in civil association) is much more than an ordering principle. It promotes rationality, helps conquer evil. Building the Kingdom is its legitimate function.[7]

Boff recognizes that this model of the Church is too closely united with modern society: How many technological advances have lived up to expectations? Has progress in one area not often come at the expense of regression in another? Has optimism halted the parade of evil—wars, genocide, environmental degradation, and grinding poverty in the midst of affluence?

Furthermore, this model shows the Church's accommodation to society, for the values and vision which it adopts are basically those of powerful people who have a comfortable place in the modern world. The Church's relationship to the outcasts of society is seen in a way that does not challenge the status quo of those who are already powerful: "the rich will be called upon to aid in the cause of the poor but without necessarily requiring a change in social class practices."[8]

People-hood and Justice for All

After examining the three historical models of the Church in Latin America, Leonardo Boff calls for a fourth, new model, drawn from his experiences in the Brazilian basic ecclesial communities. This model of the Church would be much more participatory and would avoid centralization and domination. It would be democratic, and it would emphasize the community more than the individual.[9]

Behind Boff's model is liberation theology's concern for the loss of "people-hood" in Latin America and in much of the world. In the Bible, liberation theologians remind us, God has a chosen *people*.[10] He loves the poor, the oppressed, and the landless—as a *group*. He hates the oppressors—as a *group*. To punish the enslavers, not only the firstborn of the Pharaoh but all of the firstborn of Egypt must die (Ex. 11:5).[11] In the wilderness, the sins of the fathers affect the children. Likewise, salvation comes to the community as a whole. It is the *people* who leave the Wasteland and enter into the Promised Land.[12]

Note also Israel's confession recorded in Deuteronomy 26:5–10. Although the generation of Israelites who had actually come from Egypt had passed away, their children and their grandchildren repeated the history of Egyptian oppression and God's salvation in the first person:

> And the Egyptians treated *us* harshly, and afflicted *us*, and laid upon *us* hard bondage. Then *we* cried to the Lord the God of *our* fathers, and the Lord heard *our* voice, and saw *our* affliction, *our* toil, and *our* oppression; and the Lord brought *us* out of Egypt with a mighty hand.[13]

The new wave of Latin American theologians couple their critique of "individual Christianity" with an affirmation of the importance of sharing in a broader concept of what it means to be a "people of God."[14] One of the threshold events of the Exodus occurred when that motley collection of slaves and other low-caste Semites and toilers of varying extraction, the Hebrews, began to see themselves more fully as a nation. Joshua 24 relates something of that foundation covenant when the people joined together and, with an act of faith, vowed to serve the Lord.

Basic to taking possession of the Promised Land was making a commitment to "put away the foreign gods which are among you" and to serve Yahweh.

Baalism's Real Evil

The Judeo-Christian meaning of liberation is clarified by some attention to Baal, the most active "foreign god" of the Canaanite pantheon.[15] According to Canaanite mythology, Baal was killed by another god, Mot or "Death." The earth dried up and winter set in. But Anath, Baal's sister and consort, killed Mot and restored Baal to life. This resurrection, in turn, renewed nature.

To the Canaanites, fertility of the land depended upon sexual relations between Baal and Anath. The copulation of the gods produced new life in the spring and ended the barrenness of the winter. Baal worship consisted of reenacting the mating of the gods. Through orgiastic rites with sacred prostitutes, the worshipers thought themselves to be assuring the rhythmic cycle of nature by reminding the gods of their responsibility to mate. The cult sought to control Baal, to keep nature fertile, and to maintain harmony in nature.

Beyond that, Baal religion was used as a tool by the aristocracy to maintain the social order, the status quo. Canaanite tenants worked as dispossessed farmers on estates owned by magnates, the temple, and the king. They worshiped the landowners, the baals, who not only held dominion over the land but who also held dominion over the worshipers themselves — that is, the peasants. For the baals, it was a most convenient and satisfactory system.

Old Testament criticisms of Baalism are not mere exhortations to be faithful to a competing deity. More critically, they emphasize the proper way to worship Yahweh: by acting with mercy and justice toward one's fellow humans.[16] Because justice does not prevail when some, like the baals, claim the land and its bounty while others are excluded from these privileges, Hosea chastises Israel for betraying its covenant to recognize God as the true owner of the earth. He warns that Israel, by chasing after Baal like an adulterous wife, may be punished by being returned to the wilderness, to be reminded only after hardship of the true nature of her relationship with God (Hos. 2).

In that day, Hosea writes, Israel will remember that God loves her and that his rights to the land are not only those of a baal — that is, holding the legal rights of ownership — but also those of a husband (Hos. 2:16). What Yahweh wishes is to be betrothed to his people forever in righteousness and in justice, in steadfast love, and in mercy (Hos. 2:19). These moral demands stand at the heart of his covenant with Israel (Hos. 2:21–22).

If Hosea inextricably knotted the requirements for mercy, goodness, and justice with recognition that "the earth is the Lord's and the fullness

thereof," these are even more tightly joined by the prophet Amos. Referring to the greed for possessing the land and its fruits, Amos said God is angered by those "who trample upon the needy, and bring the poor of the land to an end" (Amos 8:4). He described great landowners lying on beds of ivory (Amos 6:4–6). He talked of cows of Bashan — "fat cats" — who oppress the poor and crush the needy.

The bitter conflict that arises when some people work the land and others own it was reiterated 2,600 years after Amos's time by British economist David Ricardo. He wrote that "the interest of the landlords is always opposed to the interest of every other class in the community."[17]

Amos's indictment of Israel mentions oppression of the poor and cultic prostitution as if they were one (Amos 2:6–8). This seems strange until one recognizes that the link between these two sins is a wrongful concept of land ownership. Recall that Baal worship and its sexual rites glorified land possession and control, which were inherently inconsistent with justice. This insight was repeated much later for our age by Henry George, who wrote that "The great cause of inequality in the distribution of wealth is inequality in the ownership of land. The ownership of land is the great fundamental fact which ultimately determines the social, the political, and consequently the intellectual and moral condition of a people."[18]

Superficially this might appear as economic determinism, but George arrived from painstaking economic analysis at the conclusions reached by the prophets — namely, that the role of land is crucial in the divine providential scheme, that the flouting of just principles of land possession has grave consequences, and that human beings are caretakers, not the owners, of God's creation.

Amos and Hosea underscored that being a caretaker of the earth, while defining people's relation to the land, had a further moral dimension: It defined people's relationship to one another. Being a caretaker meant loving justice and doing mercy. Being a caretaker involved letting go of selfish possession and of the desire to have power over others by usurping their means to a livelihood, and instead becoming, like God, compassionate.

Consider what a revolutionary break this represented from Baal worship, which idolized control of the soil and deified the landowners.

A revolution in ideas and ideals, unfortunately, is not always matched by a revolution in action. The biblical scribes were not shy in reporting on the backsliding of their people. Yet, if the Israelites' flirting with the Baalism that surrounded them seems shocking, what must be said of those peoples in the present who, while seemingly far removed in time from Baalism, still, in effect, treat land monopoly as sacrosanct?

5

Poverty in the Wasteland

The "Preferential Option for the Poor" Revisited

Jesus expressed the contrast between ownership and stewardship in the pithy saying: "You cannot serve God and mammon" (Matt. 6:24; Luke 16:13). Again we see the real sting of Baal worship. Possessions, understood apart from their Creator and their usefulness to man, become "master." They become idols that dehumanize and kill. Stewardship never entails the passive acceptance of social mores that allow possessions to be masters of men (Luke 16:1–13).

Thus, being a caretaker of God's land means having a different view of reality than is prevalent in a world governed by possessions. Jesus told the parable of the Rich Man and Lazarus to greedy Pharisees to illustrate the consequences of serving mammon (Luke 16:14–31). The rich man who was inattentive to the poor man at his gate ended up in torment. Lazarus, the poor man, ended up in Abraham's bosom.

Jesus' Good News for the Oppressed

The reversal of society is the topic of Jesus' keynote address in Luke. He opens his ministry by claiming as real what Isaiah had hoped for: "The Spirit of the Lord is upon me, because He has anointed me to preach good news to the poor. He has sent me to proclaim release to the captives and ... to set at liberty those who are oppressed" (Luke 4:18).

To his followers, Jesus explains more fully that what he intends in this appropriation of Isaiah's prophecy is nothing less than a radical change of society (Luke 6:20–49). Jesus announces that the arrival of God's judgment means salvation to some and doom to others: "Happy are you who are poor"; "happy are you who are hungry"; "happy are you who are crying"; but "cursed are you who are rich"; "cursed are you who are full"; "cursed are you who are laughing" (Luke 6:20–26). The poor and the hungry can be happy because they will no longer be poor and hungry. Here, society is turned downside up.

Jesus' sermon does not stop at this announcement. He goes on to call people to stewardship.[1] He asks that men and women love their enemies; that they turn their cheeks to their assailants; and that they be merciful as God is merciful (Luke 6:27–49). These are radical demands. As the parable about the good tree bearing good fruit makes clear (Luke 6:43–45), Jesus goes beyond persuading his followers to strive for single virtues or to pursue isolated instances of charity. He urges them to do no less than act as a community where God, not mammon, rules.[2]

These social demands are much more revolutionary than are their common expressions in popular Christianity. Not only does Jesus ask people individually to be kind and generous and to lead good and useful lives, but he calls on his followers to affirm a set of corporate values which express themselves in forms that are qualitatively different from those prevailing in society—in his day or ours. How much this goes beyond the Augustinian position of a modest role for the state, or even the more activist modernist position, becomes clearer from an examination of poverty and the poor.

Not All Poor Included, Not All Rich Excluded

Latin American liberation theologians have been quick to point out that, according to the Exodus story and to Luke's gospel in particular, God's chosen people are the refuse of society.[3] The reversal—the reordering of those who are on top—is good news to the poor! But who are these poor? Why are they favored? What does this mean in terms of the Church and its relation to the state?

As already mentioned, God loves justice and mercy. This is evident when he calls out of the burning bush to Moses: "I have seen the affliction of my people who are in Egypt, and have heard their cry because of their taskmasters; I know their sufferings, and I have come down to deliver them out of the hand of the Egyptians, and to bring them up out of that land to a good and broad land, a land flowing with milk and honey" (Exod. 3:7–8). Note that God's mercy is more than the "feeling of sympathy" which many display at the sight of oppression. He sends Moses to liberate the Hebrews, and he acts in behalf of an entire people.[4]

To fathom why the Bible is said to imply a divine bias in favor of the poor, it is useful to inquire who God acts for and who he acts against.[5]

In the history of Egyptian bondage, Exodus 3, the answer seems at first blush too simple. God acts for the oppressed and against the oppressors. The oppressed are helpless to liberate themselves; the oppressors are those who dehumanize them. In other parts of the Bible, God clearly acts for the helpless—the lame, the blind, the sick, women, and children.

The recipients of God's grace, however, are not always helpless. The patriarchs, the judges, the Roman centurions, and many others in the biblical records were not helpless. They were considerably more powerful than most of their compatriots. Why, then, did God act on their behalf?

The answer is found in another attribute of God: He is faithful. God acts favorably for those who respond to him. Paul phrased this nicely when he proclaimed that "the good news is the power of God for salvation to everyone who has faith" (Rom. 1:16).

Of course, these two groups—the helpless and those who trust God—often run together in much of the Bible. And when Jesus said, "How hard it is for those who have riches to enter the kingdom of God" (Luke 18:24; Matt. 19:23; Mark 10:23), he was stating the converse, that those who are not helpless are often most lacking in faith, too. Those with wealth are so tempted to be overconfident in themselves and their possessions that they find it difficult to trust in God. Although wealth poses these difficulties, they are not insuperable. Thus Zacchaeus, who is rich, finds salvation (Luke 19:1–10).

On the other hand, not all helpless people are open to God. Luke recounts how some lepers call out for Jesus to have mercy on them and are healed. Ten lepers are cleansed, but only one returns praising God and giving thanks. It is to him that Jesus says, "Your faith has saved you" (Luke 17:19).

To his great credit, Gustavo Gutiérrez has always insisted in maintaining "both the universality of God's love and God's predilection for those on the lowest rung of the ladder of history. To focus exclusively on the one or the other is to mutilate the Christian message."[6] The Church's "preferential option for the poor"—much cited in Catholic proclamations in the United States as well as in Latin America—is misconstrued unless it is seen as an application of the injunction to do justice and love mercy.

Different Paths to Poverty

Insofar as the poor are poor *because they are victims of injustice*, Christians have an obligation not merely to correct particular instances of injustice, but also to seek to remove the structures of injustice—that is, the institutions or practices that promote oppression—from society.

Carrying out this obligation to rectify social injustice means enforcing people's rights—a political function ultimately resting upon the licit power of coercion. When oppressive special interests will not yield to moral suasion (and they seldom do) or to other means of peaceful pressure, the strong arm of the law must do its work. What if special interests control the law (as they all too frequently do in some Latin American nations and elsewhere around the globe) and if no peaceful avenues of change are open? Then armed revolution may be justified, provided always that this is not likely to lead to worse injustice — a proviso overlooked, to their eventual sorrow, by many idealistic supporters of revolution, from eighteenth-century France to contemporary Cuba and Iran.

But not all poor are poor because of injustice, structural or otherwise. Some are poor *because they are victims of bad luck.* Perhaps they inherited unfavorable genes; perhaps they were rendered destitute by natural catastrophes; perhaps the illness of loved ones plunged them into hopeless debt. Do these poor possess claims that ought to be enforced as a matter of right? No. One wants to ease their pain, but it is not from justice but from mercy that the Christian bias toward these poor stems.[7]

A good case can be made that licit physical coercion may be addressed solely to the implementation of justice. The extirpation of injustice is a function quite sufficient in itself to occupy the full attention of government as a coercive agency. (This is not to say that government action is *necessarily* coercive. As a monopoly of physical force, government is *distinctively* coercive, and in this aspect, justice is its only appropriate function. But it may also function in other, nondistinctive aspects, as when it simply administers cooperative activities. The arguments for and against its so doing are purely utilitarian and situational.) And it is not inconceivable that, with structural injustices extirpated, nongovernmental agencies and individuals could deal adequately with such poverty as might remain. That the churches have a direct and unambiguous role to play as engines of humanitarian relief is, of course, beyond question. It is what they, of all agencies, do best.

A third category of the poor are those who are poor *because of their own sloth or improvidence.* What was said about the poor whose poverty springs from bad luck applies yet more strongly to them: They possess no claims that ought to be enforced as a matter of right. They, too, are to be embraced within the scope of Christian mercy. But it is a false benevolence that does not incorporate safeguards against perpetuating and encouraging the very vices that brought about their wretchedness. To aid such persons at the risk of imposing poverty upon industrious and thrifty citizens is itself a form of injustice, which is further reason why such aid, ideally, should be voluntary.

Were these three causes of poverty mutually exclusive, designing an antipoverty strategy would be infinitely simpler. But in practice a given pauper may be, all at the same time, a victim of injustice, bad luck, and his own vices. Certainly the first priority of society, then, is to seek to abolish injustice through the use of law and, where necessary in extreme situations, to work outside the law to change the law. But society should be more cautious than it typically has been to avoid creating new injustices when it uses the power of government to soften the buffets of ill-fortune or to assuage the penalties of vice.

Devising policies to help the worthy poor is not the end of the problem. Concern over the marginalized implies that the worthy poor should have the material power and wealth they now lack. If these poor acquire power and wealth, what is to keep them from becoming, like the unworthy rich, exploiters of another set of poor people?

Spiritual blindness, as already noted, often attends the possession of material power and wealth. The story of the rich young ruler (Matt. 19:16–26) underscores their snares, and it is not without reason that Catholic religious orders have required vows of poverty and that "worldly asceticism" has been a hallmark of the Calvinist ethic. Smug complacency and preoccupation with meaningless fripperies are peculiar temptations that make faith difficult for the wealthy. For those whose wealth has become for them an idol, the Church's call to voluntary renunciation is not misplaced.

Yet involuntary poverty is scarcely any guarantee of faith. If it were, its promotion ought to be a primary mission of evangelism, and the exploitation of the disadvantaged a cause to make the Church rejoice.

True, the poor are not apt to be overly preoccupied with actual involvement in "the good life," since it is outside their reach. And the powerless can scarcely be faulted for abuse of power or for failure to use it worthily. But their condition nevertheless has its own spiritual pitfalls.

First, the struggle for bare survival may absorb their whole attention, reducing them to the psychic status of mere brutes. The sardonic aphorism of Brecht's Macheath, "*Erst kommt das Fressen, dann kommt die Moral*" (roughly, "first you fatten your belly, then you think of morality"), may be applied not only to ethics but to everything that elevates human life. Possibly the most damning indictment of structural injustice is the way in which it tends to stultify its prey, rendering him "A thing that grieves not and that never hopes, Stolid and stunned, a brother to the ox."[8]

Second, the poor are signally vulnerable to the soul-destroying acids of envy and *ressentiment*. (This is not to deny that these acids also may corrode the lives of the affluent, as witness those who, surrounded by comforts, nevertheless become obsessed with striving to "keep up with the Joneses.") Particularly is this so in our consumerist culture, fed on every hand by advertising and television depictions of the sybaritic lifestyles of the rich. According to Nietzsche, Christianity's glorification of meekness and self-denial is but an expression of the *ressentiment* felt by the weak and poor, who, in making a virtue of their necessity, by implication locate evil in strength and plenitude. While we consider this a misreading of genuine Christianity, we reluctantly concede it to be a penetrating account of the motives of many who consider themselves Christians.

Finally, the poor are understandably susceptible to escapist models of religion that are sorry counterfeits of an authentic faith that follows Christ because of what he is in himself, rather than because he is seen as a means to "pie in the sky." This tendency is natural, and we can view it sympathetically when it characterizes those who have no hope of getting even a modest share of earthly pie. Yet it does not invest the poor with dignity or make them vessels of divine insight.

Romanticizing and Charity Fail to Liberate

Liberation theologians and other social reformers often fall into the trap of romanticizing the poor. As Nicolas Berdyaev wryly recalled from his demi-Marxist phase:

I then thought that the proletariat, as a working and class-conscious group, exploited but at the same time free from the sin of exploitation, possessed the psychological structure that is favorable to the revelation of truth; that in it psychological consciousness, as it were, coincided with the transcendental consciousness. . . . I have since greatly departed from the ideological concepts of my youth.[9]

The temptation of thinking of God's bias for the poor in terms of a higher spirituality brought about by poverty needs to be resisted. Powerlessness does not in itself signify holiness.

The issue is complex. If the poor may often be described as stunted, envious, resentful, and escapist, note that this is how they react impotently to exploitation insofar as they are unable to organize and give coherence to their own needs and interests. Liberation theology at its best has been an effort to build and reinforce such new modes of thought and action-oriented linkage among the poor as may enable them to overcome both oppression without and psychological deformity within. To that effect, Gustavo Gutiérrez, Leonardo Boff, and other liberation theologians stress that the bias for the poor in the Bible goes beyond a well-meant concern for deprived people.[10]

The biblical bias can be traced back to the nature of God himself. God, finally, is the one who rejects power and takes upon himself, in the person of his son, the ultimate sacrifice in solidarity with all who are crucified by the power structures of this world. He not only has compassion for the poor, but becomes, like them, weak. God reverses society, true—but more, he appears on the cross as a manifestation of this reversal. As Paul expressed so vividly, God appears as foolishness, a stumbling block, weakness, and moreover, he uses "what is low and despised in the world . . . to bring to nothing things that are" (1 Cor. 1:18–31).

To assert that God "rejects power" and "becomes weak" is clearly not the same thing as asserting that he is weak inherently. His weakness must be seen, rather, as related to his will to become one with his people. He wishes to be worshiped genuinely for the sake of his agapeic essence, not falsely for the sake of attributes which compel, out of fear, a counterfeit of worship. Thus Christ, in Dostoyevsky's powerful symbolism, spurns the Devil's temptation to make use of miracle, mystery, and authority, inviting instead a faith that finds in Truth and Goodness their own intrinsic validation.[11] It is in this sense that Jesus said, "My kingdom is not of this world"

(John 18:36), for in this world predatory power assails the innocent and must be contained and curbed by power harnessed to their defense.

"I have overcome the world" (John 16:33) may be interpreted to mean that Truth and Goodness are triumphant simply because of what they are and that nothing external can affect them. But

> [h]uman life and freedom cannot be made to depend entirely upon the spiritual condition of other men, society and its rulers. The rights of the individual must be safeguarded in case that spiritual condition proves to be a low one or not sufficiently enlightened by grace. A society that chose to be based solely upon grace and declined to have any law would be a despotic society. . . . It is impossible to wait for a gracious regeneration of society to make human life bearable.[12]

As a citizen of the spiritual order, the Christian lives under grace and is not constrained by power or authority. But in this life he is also, inescapably, a citizen of the secular order, where power must be checked by power and political means employed to serve the ends of grace, moving the world closer to a likeness of the Promised Land.

In a book entitled *The True Church and the Poor*, Jon Sobrino has argued for a new vision of the Church, not as an instrument *for* the poor, but as a body which understands its very nature and derives its categories from the experience of the poor, a Church *of* the poor.[13] His dominant insight is significant: Clearly God does not wish to act in such a way that keeps the poor poor. Occasional charity does not accomplish enough. God also does not wish to act in such a way that the poor are treated as second-class citizens who need to be looked after as wards by religious paternalists. Rather, God acts to end poverty. This good news to the poor may be perceived differently by the rich.

The Promised Land means, among other things, an end to the causes of oppression. That is why liberation theologians such as Sobrino affirm a political stance for the Church. If sin and salvation have a social, corporate dimension, then the Church must be concerned with the structures of society — certainly not excluding the laws and customs concerning the ownership and tenure of land.[14]

Thus, liberationists and theologians of whatever camp who seek to move civilization out of the Wasteland and into the Promised Land must ask: How can we deinstitutionalize poverty built upon a baal view of the land? Finding answers to this question would indeed be "good news to the poor."

6

Suffering in the Wasteland

Independence — But Still Wandering in the Wilderness

It is easy to see parallels between the oppression in colonial Latin America and in Pharaoh's Egypt. In both cases, the peasants were exploited by an aristocracy that believed itself divinely entitled to the land and its fruits, an arrangement supported by the official religion. It is also easy, from our vantage point in history, to identify various causes of the oppression: an elitist view of government; a moral code based on power; a society insensitive to basic human rights; hard-hearted rulers; arbitrary laws. One can almost see the afflictions of the people and hear their cries.

More difficult, perhaps, is to try to comprehend the suffering that has occurred *after* independence. Again, the parallel with the Hebrews in the Old Testament is instructive. After the exodus from Egypt but long before the people crossed the Jordan, they complained to Moses: "Why have you made us come out of Egypt, to bring us to this evil place? It is no place for grain, or figs, or vines, or pomegranates; and there is no water to drink" (Num. 20:5).

This complaining, as mentioned earlier, arising from an erosion of faith, was partly responsible for the Hebrews' forty-year exile in the wilderness. They were, of course, in error in blaming God for their suffering and in assuming that freedom would be (or is ever) cheaply gained. But this is not to deny that their suffering itself was real.

Likewise, the suffering in Latin America today, two hundred years after the movements of independence, is real. The oppression is not always of exactly the same type as in colonial times, but people are hungry and too many are unable to provide healthy, decent lives for their children.

Significantly, the transition zone — the Wasteland — is a disturbing place. After escaping their captors, the Hebrews were even hungrier than they had been in Egypt. Once they could no longer blame their suffering on bad people, wrong decisions, and aberrant ideas, the Hebrews felt the over-whelming power of the Wasteland.

Sometimes the causes of hunger and death cannot be attributed either to a "Pharaoh who knew not Joseph" or to the personal failures or mere ill luck of the individuals who hunger and die. Against this backdrop, under-standing the destructive forces of an oppressive environment, the South American liberation theologians charge European and North American theologians with having been too quick to interiorize evil.[1] They react against the historical view (discussed in chapter 4) that sin applies to indi-viduals only, not to governments.

People in our times have placed such emphasis on how evil stems from and affects the individual that they have almost lost the sense of evil as a phenomenon of social institutions, organizations, and structures. This applies across the religious spectrum. The fundamentalist typically speaks of evil as something that *individuals* can bypass or choose to avoid. And the liberal typically speaks of evil as something that *individuals* can conquer or choose to do away with.

Returning to the Wasteland metaphor, a people may be caught in a place without sufficient food or water. There they cannot relieve their suf-fering merely through individuals seeking to behave properly. (This has been a major theme in the works of Garrett Hardin.) To survive they must change society's ground rules, such a monumental undertaking that it may be said to require God's special intervention.

This critical shift from problems caused by evil leaders to the oppression caused by large impersonal forces is not limited to Latin America or par-ticular nations. Liberationists point, for example, to male-dominated social *structures* that dehumanize women. They describe the extent to which blacks, Hispanics, and other minorities suffer from hidden agendas embed-ded within *institutions*, almost unseen by the majority. They remind us how a military-industrial complex, multinational corporation, government bureau, giant banking center, or other powerful *organization* may deper-sonalize citizens, depriving them of effective control over their own lives.[2]

Because some of the most oppressive institutions are those that govern land policy, it is necessary to examine how the economics of evil has been addressed by liberation theologians. In the discourse of Latin American liberation theology, neocolonialism *is* the Wasteland.

Economic Development and Dependency

The 1950s was the decade of developmentalism. It was an optimistic time. Underdevelopment and development were said to be on a continuum, the one leading to the other, and Latin America was seen on the verge of achieving self-sustained economic growth. Using nations such as the United States, England, and Germany as models, underdeveloped nations supposedly could copy their steps into industrialization and surge forward to prosperity.

Pope Paul VI questioned this promise of economic development in his 1967 encyclical, *Populorum Progressio*.[3] He saw rich nations developing quickly while poor nations developed slowly. He saw discord between people and nations arising from glaring worldwide inequalities of power and possessions.

These conflicts arose in part, the Pope said, from too narrowly conceiving development as limited to economic growth. He called for broadening the goal to promote the good of every person, with emphasis on the whole person. Development should not only provide necessities and end misery, but also pursue an increase of knowledge and culture, esteem for the dignity of others, peace and cooperation, and, in sum, it should seek "for each and all the transition from less human conditions to those which are more human."[4] Paul VI mentioned two guideposts for achieving these goals. First, the right of private property should not be absolute and unconditional.[5] At times, for the common good, it is necessary to expropriate private property.[6] Second, a system that operates on the bases of "profit as the key motive for economic progress, competition as the supreme law of economics, and private ownership of the means of production as an absolute right that has no limits or social obligations" should be replaced by an economy at the service of man.[7]

In *Populorum Progressio*, Paul VI identified himself with the poor nations of the world. He decried the fact that whole populations live in a state of dependency, destitute of necessities and cut off from initiative, social responsibility, and cultural advancement.

The encyclical was vague in parts, not explaining, for instance, how "an economy at the service of man" comes into being. It shied away from radical solutions, apparently trusting that powerful people and institutions could be persuaded to act for the common good. It blamed much of the disequilibrium between rich and poor nations on free trade, which Paul VI assumed was unjustly putting poor countries at further disadvantage.[8] The document nevertheless served to correct a popular belief that economic growth alone is a sufficient path toward progress and dramatized how poor nations may be held captive by their economic dependence on rich ones.

The Center and the Periphery

Four years later, Gustavo Gutiérrez raised a more substantive critique of development theory in his epochal work, *A Theology of Liberation*.[9] He charged that the push for development, while raising expectations, had not succeeded in breaking the hold of economic stagnation because development theory did not address the roots of the situation.

As he saw it, underdevelopment, instead of being a step on the way to progress, is really a by-product of development; it is the historical end process of the economic expansion of great capitalist countries.[10] Rich countries stood at the center and poor countries at the periphery of a closed system. The amount of fat of wealthy nations was directly related to the amount of hunger among poor nations.

Further, Gutiérrez claimed that Third World development was promoted by organizations closely linked to control of the world's economy.[11] That was why their policies did not challenge the control mechanisms. They devised strategies which kept the weak countries economically, socially, politically, and culturally dependent on the powerful countries. The dynamics of world economics dictated the simultaneous perpetuation of great poverty for the many and the creation of great wealth for the few.[12]

To break away from this aspect of the world economy, Gutiérrez saw the need for a radical departure from the status quo. He appropriated the biblical language of liberation that, for three thousand years now, has been the idiom of oppressed people and captives. Thus, the first step toward a new society must be to sever the *bondage* of dependence.

Gutiérrez did not purport to be stating anything original. He simply advanced, in a theological context — as in a somewhat more restricted way the Medellín conference of Latin American bishops had done in 1968 — ideas drawn from the "dependency theory" school of secular Latin American social scientists. Among those whose work he cited were Andre Gunder Frank and Fernando Henrique Cardoso. Frank's version of dependency theory is a variation on the Leninist doctrine of imperialism (itself borrowed largely from John A. Hobson); Cardoso's version is more moderate.[13] Gutiérrez sided with Cardoso in rejecting a monocausal interpretation of dependence, yet insisted that the analysis be "put within the framework of the worldwide class struggle."[14] In more recent writings, his endorsement of dependency theory has become increasingly qualified.[15] For instance, in "Expanding the View," Gutiérrez cites dependency theory as an example of "an inadequate tool" used when liberation theologians had initially adopted a "simplistic position" in analyzing the situation of poverty.[16]

So too with other liberation theologians. Friar Leonardo Boff, for instance, concedes that dependency theory is "only a theory, not an established truth,"[17] and Arthur McGovern, who has written a sympathetic assessment of liberation theology, cautions that liberation theology "needs to weigh legitimate criticisms against those dependency arguments that oversimplify causes and solutions."[18] On the other hand, Rubem Alves, the earliest of the liberation theologians (although he declines to call himself one), author of a book entitled, ironically, *A Theology of Human Hope*, now despairs of structural change. He has adopted what he calls an "eschatological" stance, as if awaiting the Last Judgment to set things straight, so strongly has he come to believe that the periphery is impotent in the face of overwhelming domination by the center.[19]

A Stance against Free Trade

The censorious attitude displayed in *Populorum Progressio* toward free trade is even more pronounced in dependency theory. Sometimes it takes the form, as with Raul Prebisch, of a yearning for autarky—of agitation, that is, for complete self-sufficiency by substituting local products for imports. This is not an unnatural response for those who believe their countrymen to be helpless pawns of international financial conspiracies or of ruthless pressures emanating from distant nuclei of economic power. In Latin America this tradition reaches back at least to Francia, dictator of Paraguay from 1816 to 1840, who enforced a national policy of almost total isolation.

Sometimes antipathy to free trade avoids this pursuit of withdrawal into isolation. It is then heard as a call for economic intercourse, not through the usual avenues of trade or investment, but through wealth sharing on the part of the developed world, a call that may be couched in terms of reparations.

This is not the place for a thoroughgoing analysis of international trade. But a solid body of opinion now holds that "protective" trade barriers tend to violate personal liberty, decrease the production of wealth, favor special interests at the expense of the general population, and lead to wasteful duplication by interfering with the normal tendency of each nation to specialize in what it is capable of doing best.

Moreover, close scrutiny reveals that the supposed ill effects often attributed to free trade result not from the unhindered flow of commerce per se but rather from various forms of legalized piracy. These deprive buyers and sellers of a fair exchange, whether their trade is domestic or across national borders. For this reason, one of the most rigorous polemics ever launched against the fallacies of protectionism[20] concludes with a demonstration that free trade, however desirable in itself, can do little to elevate the condition of the needy without a further and more basic measure: the resolution of the land question. Any nation, rich or poor, that accomplishes this can then fully enjoy the benefits of free trade. Natural or cultural factors may still keep it *relatively* poor, but its people will obtain more for their labor once their ability to spend their earnings as they like is unrestricted.

Cracks in Dependency Theory

Trade policy aside, dependency theory does focus on the reality of dreadful poverty. It would be fatuous not to admit that some of Latin America's poverty is traceable historically to the operations of First World companies and to the interventions of First World governments, as the theory holds. However, the following points indicate that dependency theory is off the mark in important respects, rendering it of questionable value as the key to a solution, as Gutiérrez and Boff now recognize, or even as a diagnostic tool.[21]

For most of the past three decades, Latin America experienced vigorous and sustained economic growth. While all social groups did not benefit proportionally, the middle class expanded. There was decided improvement in the education of even the least-advantaged groups. The percentage, although unfortunately not the number, of persons living in poverty has been reduced.[22]

Life expectancy, a fairly reliable proxy for health and quality of life, increased for all classes. This of course also has a negative side: longer life spans, combined with a soaring birthrate, create new pressures on the Latin American economy. Pressures on the housing supply are one example. But such pressures can in no sense be attributed to the dependency of poor nations on rich nations.[23]

Dependency persists, but this does not automatically justify the charge that it stems chiefly from exploitation of the periphery by the center.[24] Jumping to this conclusion assumes a zero-sum situation where one region can increase its wealth only at the expense of reducing wealth in another region. This overlooks evidence that the quantity of the world's wealth is not static but is constantly being magnified by human enterprise.[25] Some implications of this fact are illustrated in the cases of Canada and Albania.

United States investment in Canada is significantly greater than in all of Latin America. Many Canadian nationalists view their county as a "U.S. colony," economically speaking. Yet Canada's standard of living is among the world's highest, due in no small measure to the trade and investment which, were dependency theory correct, should have had the opposite effect.

By contrast, Albania is among the least dependent of nations in the contemporary era. Until recently it neither traded nor maintained diplomatic relations, even with other Marxist states. This isolation from great trading powers, far from liberating Albania's people, leaves them as the poorest and most wretched nation in Europe.

The theory of dependency, in Gutiérrez's words, "does not take sufficient account of the internal dynamics of each country or of the vast dimensions of the world of the poor."[26] Dependency and underdevelopment seem to result at least as much, and usually a great deal more, from domestic factors than from those imposed by outsiders. These domestic factors include cultural habits and traditions, but especially political structures and institutions that combine to inhibit economic creativity, discourage local investment, and provide impetus for the flight of capital to more hospitable and stable havens.[27]

Highlighting the paramount importance of these domestic factors is the remarkable transformation over the past two decades of several Asian Pacific Rim countries—notably Japan, South Korea, Taiwan, Hong Kong, and Singapore. They have undergone spectacular economic growth, multiplying their respective national wealth over 1,000 percent and rapidly elevating the level of their poor. Meagerly endowed with natural resources, these countries were, moreover, devastated economically by World War II. Their populations entered the period after 1945 in a state of poverty more extreme than that of Latin America, and South Korea was further ravaged by the Korean War. Today, Japan stands second among all nations in gross national product, and the other East Asian countries mentioned have left the Third World to join the ranks of "developed" nations in terms both of the vigor of their economies and of the prosperity of their peoples.

The reasons for this dramatic turnaround are often said to be certain native traditions such as social discipline, family savings (as opposed to high spending and indebtedness), and great respect for literacy. Without in any way denigrating these attributes, it must be noted that they were present before the economic rejuvenation occurred. What released the potency of these aspects of their cultures?

These nations in the postwar era drastically revised structural features such as tax, trade, land, and regulatory policies in ways that promoted initiative, rewarded production, and prescribed a fairer distribution of wealth. Interestingly, according to Frank, the basis of "metropolitan monopoly over the satellites" (domination of the center over the periphery) has shifted from heavy industry to technology. Yet these East Asian states managed, thanks to the structural features just mentioned, to break out of the periphery by doing what he regards as "difficult and unlikely" — developing competitive technology.[28]

Even insofar as dependency theory is (in a limited sense) analytically correct, the social ills to which it calls attention could be substantially dispelled by the proper allocation of rent or land values. (How such allocation can be done is addressed in some detail in chapter 9.) This is highlighted by an analysis of how Third World exploitation operates. Corporations, says David Richards, "suck away the primary wealth of the peripheries" in several ways. When, as is often the case, they enjoy virtually tax-free land, these firms retain the land rent for the greater profit of their stockholders back in North America, Britain, Japan, or wherever. They often pass the misappropriated land rent on in the form of lower prices to customers who reside largely outside South and Central America. When corporations are charged a genuine rent for the resources and locations they use, payments are usually made to the "periphery's land-owning oligarchies . . . which then spend it on imports from the centre."[29]

Is it not evident that if the poorer nations collected for their own people the bulk of the mammoth land rent funds that are now siphoned off in these ways, this would strike a telling blow at their impoverishment?

7

Detours in the Wilderness

Marxism and Liberation

The children of Israel did not take a direct route to the Promised Land. Instead, following a pillar of cloud by day and of fire by night, they made for Sinai, where the Law was delivered to Moses on the mountaintop. It was about a year and three months after fleeing Egypt that they left Sinai (Num. 10:11–13). Still led by the miraculous pillar of cloud and fire, they headed northeast to the Wilderness of Paran. There, contrary to the divine command to proceed on to the Promised Land, they gave credence to the pusillanimous counsel of the spies who intimidated them with reports of the might of its inhabitants. Ignoring the pleas of Joshua and Caleb, they murmured in rebellion, thinking to return to Egypt. For this they were subjected to a terrible reproof and penalty: "Your carcasses shall fall in this wilderness . . . according to your whole number from twenty years and upward . . . save Caleb and Joshua. . . . And your children shall wander in the wilderness forty years" (Num. 14:29–33; Num. 32:8–14).

After this we read no more of their being shown the way by pillars of cloud and fire. They spent the next four decades meandering aimlessly in the vicinity of Kadesh. Their leader, Moses, was a notable spiritual guide, but evidently no geographer.

So, too, such liberation theologians as Gutiérrez are authentic spiritual leaders. But it may be argued that they have tended, as in their use of dependency theory, to rely on many a false compass when it comes to socioeconomic guidance.

Besides dependency theory, other instruments that seem to point in wrong directions for reaching the liberating goal of a just society—the Promised Land—are the concept of *alienation*, the theory of *surplus value*, the doctrine of *class struggle*, and *socialism*. Each of these will be treated in turn. All, like some versions of dependency theory, are aspects of Marxian thought, although the concept of alienation was not considered orthodox within the Soviet bloc, and socialism is an ideal by no means limited to Marxists. Not all of these positions have been maintained by every liberation theologian, Latin American or otherwise. In fact, a few liberationists such as José Comblin have strongly criticized Marxism;[1] many others, like Jon Sobrino, have avoided using Marxist categories. Moreover, full-orbed Marxism also embraces other teachings, most notably atheism and historical materialism, which all Christian liberation theologians necessarily reject.[2]

Nobody who reads Gutiérrez, its most important and influential representative almost from the beginning, could reasonably dismiss liberation theology as ever having been a mere "smoke screen for Marxism," regardless of the statements and affiliations of some of its exponents. His books are permeated with doctrinally impeccable expressions of evangelical Christianity, thoroughly Chalcedonian in their Christology, testifying of God's transcendence and of his unmerited, salvific grace in history.[3]

To say that liberation theologians have, in varying degree, been influenced by aspects of Marxism does not, of course, imply that they are, even in these aspects, slavish devotees of Marx, or that they have not also been open to insights from other secular movements such as Freudianism, existentialism, and phenomenology. Nor does it signify that Marxism is a monolithic system allowing for no differences of interpretation; on two occasions Marx himself stated: "All I know is that I am not a Marxist."[4] The complexity of his thought, his changes in emphasis and terminology, the opacity of his style, and the sheer volume of his output (much of which was never published in his lifetime, perhaps in some instances because of his own dissatisfaction with it), not to mention the distinctive cast added by Engels, his collaborator and posthumous editor, have given rise to massive problems of exegesis and led to endless conflicts, even among those who count themselves his orthodox adherents.

The purpose of this chapter is not to present a definitively "correct" exposition of Marx's thought (although every effort has been made to avoid misrepresenting it), but to confront Marxist themes that often have affected and distorted the socioeconomic outlook of liberation theologians.

Twenty years after the seminal 1968 conference of Latin American bishops in Medellín, Colombia, which gave its blessing to many key liberationist ideas, a *New York Times* writer pointed out that liberation theologians "continue to employ Marxist concepts . . . but with increasing reservations," and that dependency theory, Marxist or otherwise, has lost some of its vogue among them.[5] Presumably the flood of criticism from persons who are now unmuzzled, after enduring decades of Communist economic policies, is raising further doubts among intellectual leaders, and Marxist influence has become increasingly attenuated. If what follows in this chapter therefore seems somewhat anachronistic, we feel nevertheless compelled to include it, partly on historical grounds, but more importantly because Marxist analysis, however toned down, still retains a measure of vitality in liberationist thinking.[6]

Alienation: The Worker as Subhuman Machine

Alienation is a concept co-opted by the youthful Marx from Feuerbach's critique of Hegelian idealism and, to some degree, from Hegel's own *Phenomenology of Spirit*. "By 'alienation' Marx meant, in general terms, that the projections of human experience in thought or social institutions are misleadingly separated from man in abstract speculation and acquire a harmful power over him in his social life, dividing him from himself and his fellow men so that he is never truly whole and never truly 'at home.' "[7] In 1844, Marx had come to apply this notion more particularly to economic relationships, claiming that under capitalism and the profit system (i.e., production of commodities — goods made for exchange rather than for direct use), persons become enslaved by things, and their labor "appears as torment" to them. By overturning the profit system, man can free himself from alienation and live on a genuinely human plane.

It is easy to see the appeal of these ideas to those who propound a theology of liberation. But Marx's economic determinism came to be increasingly rigid and all-encompassing, a tendency carried still further by Engels. According to the "idealistic" or "humanistic" concept of alienation (which is favored by liberationists), the determinism is but proximate: Man is determined by economic relationships only because and to the extent that he allows himself to be. The economic order is his creation, and he can alter it to be his servant rather than his master.

However, it is doubtful that Marx ever held the view that man can change himself and his economic environment simply by an act of will. As early as 1844, he and Engels asserted, in opposition to the Young Hegelian "fantasy" that men's relationships and limitations are products of their consciousness, that "the nature of individuals ... depends on the material conditions which determine their production."[8] This implies that labor must remain alienated until the economic order is overturned, which will take place only when the time is ripe — i.e., when the fully developed capitalist mode of commodity production has created a self-conscious revolutionary proletariat which embraces the "immense majority" of the population — a position made explicit four years later in *The Communist Manifesto*.[9] Thus, human destiny reflects a historically inevitable dialectical progression of modes of production and exchange; economic determinism is ultimate in the sense that it alone produces the necessary preconditions for its own transcendence.

It would appear as if Marx found the source of alienation in exchange itself. When production for direct use gives way to production for exchange (commodity production), human relations cease to be convivial and become commercial. Instead of controlling the products of his labor, the worker becomes dominated by them as they take on an existence independent of and hostile to him: The more he produces, the less he has to consume; the more beautiful or powerful the product, the more dwarfish and impotent is he, and so forth. Instead of fully and spontaneously affirming himself in his labor, the worker denies himself. His work becomes external to him, the property of someone else, not the satisfaction of an inner need, but only a *means* of satisfying other needs. Instead of realizing his humanity in man's distinctive "essence" or "life-activity"—work—the individual whose labor is but a means becomes estranged from his own being as a member of the human species. And finally, instead of seeing other individuals as persons in the fullness of their common humanity, he sees them only as bosses, competitors, or tools.[10]

In earlier stages of productive organization, although the worker may be exploited, his alienation is restrained by patriarchal associations, feudal bonds, guild restrictions, religious sanctions, and the like. Under capitalism, however, nothing stands between the individual and the market. In the wage relationship which finds its apogee in capitalism, the worker possesses formal freedom to exchange his labor power as a commodity, unhampered by constraints of status. All is reduced to the "cash nexus"—the instrument and symbol of free contract and equality before the law. But the market becomes to him a tyrant worse than any oriental despot, an overwhelming, impersonal, anarchic force which neither he nor his employers are able to predict, control, or understand.[11]

The wage relationship, as a feature of the process of exchange, partakes of the alienating character of that process. Labor power is bought and sold as a commodity. Once a contract has been entered into, formal equality between buyer and seller disappears. The buyer becomes master, and the seller, servant: "He, who before was the money owner, now strides in front as capitalist; the possessor of labour-power follows as his labourer. The one with an air of importance, smirking, intent on business; the other, timid and holding back, like one who is bringing his own hide to market and has nothing to expect but—a hiding."[12]

The division of labor is, according to Marx, another alienating feature of the process of exchange, especially in that mode of production, capitalism, which subjects all other considerations to the market. This manifests itself in its most crippling form within the factory, where the worker is confined to the repetitive performance of some simple detail operation all his working life.

Roberts and Stephenson argue convincingly that the division of labor is not, as such, for Marx the source of alienation, and will not, as he viewed it, be abolished under communism. It is a universal element of economics. Even under production for direct use, division of labor will exist, and under postcapitalist production for direct use, it will exist in complex form. But in "the higher phase of communist society," "the *enslaving subordination of the individual to the division of labour"* will be abolished,[13] even if not the division of labor itself. "The effect of detailed labor on the individual is *evaded* by a social plan that rotates the work force through the various tasks."[14]

Marx contrasted the productive efficiency of the capitalist factory as a social unit consciously organized so as to maximize output to the utmost, with what he saw as the atomistic chaos of the exchange mechanism, in which the factory (along with private individuals) participates as a discrete, uncoordinated entity. Disproportionality between production and consumption, violent price fluctuations, and chronic waste of both labor power and capital, are all, thought Marx, intrinsic to the market. Therefore, he would eliminate the market altogether: Production for exchange would be supplanted by production for direct use. However, instead of being controlled by custom and tradition, as in precapitalist stages, production for use would be controlled scientifically by central planners representing all the workers, who would be, at least in principle, coextensive with the community at large. All labor would now be socially useful labor, and all products socially useful products. In this way, the efficiency of the modern factory would be translated to the whole community, without any of its deleterious effects. The division of labor would be rendered innocuous, and specialization unnecessary, while each individual would be enabled freely to realize his full human potential as a cooperating member of a conscious, self-directed collectivity.

Alienation is thus ultimately overcome in a utopia in which "society regulates the general production, making it possible for me to do one thing today and another tomorrow, to hunt in the morning, fish in the afternoon, breed cattle in the evening, criticize after dinner, just as I like, without ever becoming a hunter, a fisherman, a herdsman or a critic."[15] This passage is not from *Alice in Wonderland*, but occurs in a work in which Marx and Engels deride the Young Hegelians for their "innocent and childlike fantasies"![16] Exactly *how* society is to regulate the general production so as to make possible such idyllic versatility, they disdain to inform us.

Non-Marxists can agree that persons should not be reduced to mere embodiments of narrow economic functions. Moreover, it may be freely granted that the division of labor has been carried to dehumanizing extremes from the early days of the Industrial Revolution to "Modern Times" as satirized by Charlie Chaplin in the movie of that name. Enlightened industries recognize that sophisticated tools can perform repetitive tasks, avoiding the mindless human specialization that tends to thwart productive efficiency rather than enhance it. Marx himself predicted this recognition as economically inevitable, and even cited manifestations of it in his time, but evidently thought that its implementation on a significant scale could only take place after the seizure of power by the working class.[17]

More will be said later about central planning, but a rhetorical question may suffice to relate it to the present topic of alienation. Let us bear in mind that every individual, whatever else, is necessarily a consumer. Is human freedom expanded or contracted, and human potential enriched or impoverished, when decisions as to what goods and services are useful and desirable are made, not by individuals in the marketplace, but by remote officials, however wise or democratically selected?

To assert that man is alienated is scarcely novel; Christianity has asserted this from the beginning. It has also recognized the role that economic factors play in alienation: To serve mammon is to cut oneself off from God (Matt. 6:24), as well as from one's fellows, and to deny one's own potential. Yet, according to Christian doctrine, alienation is not the mechanical result of economic forces; it is endemic to man's fallen state. Even the most routine, intrinsically boring labor need not be alienating if performed to the glory of God; witness much of the "menial" work of members of religious orders. Conversely, Berdyaev has pointed out that creative activity can be diabolical and dehumanizing.[18]

Moreover, as Ronald H. Nash remarks:

> Human alienation is hardly unique to capitalist societies. It is difficult to believe that a garbage collector in Moscow is any happier with his job than a garbage collector in Boston, Cleveland, or Beverly Hills. Alienation and dehumanization are serious problems, but it is simply not true that they result exclusively from conditions in capitalist societies and vanish once those societies have become socialist.[19]

Liberation theologians characteristically have identified the abolition of the profit system with the conquest of alienation, which, in turn, means the emergence of a new man—free, unselfish, creative, socially responsible— the shaper of his own destiny. It is instructive that their most massive systematic effort, a five-volume work by Juan Luis Segundo, is entitled *Theology for Artisans of a New Humanity.* "Our revolution," proclaims Miranda, "is directed toward the creation of the new human being,"[20] and Gutiérrez speaks of the "building of a *new man.*"[21] All this accords with the Marxist view that human nature is plastic and can be transformed by structurally altering material relationships. But it does not accord with the traditional Christian acknowledgment that human nature is sinful and can be transformed only through the operation of divine grace in the hearts of individuals. Nor does it account for the fact that alienation occurs in socialist as well as in capitalist societies.

Surplus Value: Pseudo-Scientific Rationale for Worker Revolt

Among liberation theologians, exploitation has been a major rallying point. Although, for Marx, exploitation of the worker is far from being unique to capitalism, it is with capitalism, in which commodity production

(production for exchange) attains its purest and most developed form, that exploitation, too, is most developed. Yet here, exploitation, instead of being seen for what it is, is "disguised under the shape of social relations between the products of labour."[22] This disguise is termed in *Capital* "the fetishism of commodities" but is certainly not without a family resemblance to alienation. It is facilitated by the use of money as a medium of exchange, which helps to render impersonal and abstract what was, in earlier modes of production, personal and concrete.

Marx recognized that capital is "stored-up" or "congealed" labor,[23] but divided it into two kinds: "constant" and "variable." Constant capital consists of such things as raw and auxiliary materials, and machinery; variable capital is capital used to purchase current labor power.

The value of the labor congealed in constant capital is, according to Marx, conveyed in the course of production to the commodity, without any increase in magnitude. But the value of the labor congealed in variable capital is not only transferred to the commodity but "also produces an excess, a surplus-value, which may itself vary, may be more or less according to circumstances."[24] This surplus he accounts for by asserting that only *current* labor creates new value,[25] while the worker is normally paid no more than "the value of the necessaries of life habitually required by the average labourer."[26]

Marx's reasoning on this central point demands further scrutiny. In the course of production for exchange, the value of any commodity is determined by the amount of labor time socially necessary for its production. In the case of labor power (viewed as a commodity under capitalism), this means the time required to permit the worker to produce his own means of subsistence and reproduction.

> But the past labour that is embodied in the labour-power, and the living labour that it can call into action; the daily cost of maintaining it, and its daily expenditure in work, are two totally different things. The former determines the exchange-value of the labour-power, the latter its use-value. ... The seller of labour-power, like the seller of any other commodity, realises its exchange-value, and parts with its use-value. He cannot take the one without giving the other."[27]

Thus the capitalist, in a hypothetical illustration advanced by Marx, is able to buy the use of a whole day's labor for the cost of only half a day's labor time, which is all that is required to sustain the worker and enable him to beget new workers.[28] The value of this extra work, translated into the exchange value of the product, is surplus value, realized as profit by the capitalist.

Inasmuch as labor time over and above what is needed to maintain labor power is extracted in modes of production in which exchange is not the dominant characteristic, a type of surplus value exists also in these modes.

But it does not display the dynamic and expansive nature of surplus value under capitalism. Since labor power is not viewed as a commodity in these modes, extraction tends to be constrained by traditional social relations of a nonmarket character. Moreover, the accumulation of surplus value by precapitalist exploiters was limited by their ability to consume use-values. Accumulation beyond what could be immediately consumed was done mainly with an eye to future consumption. But under capitalism, accumulation becomes an end in itself as an essential feature of the system. Accumulation in this mode is not a matter of mere hoarding but of the augmentation of capital through exchange, and stems not from simple greed but from the structural necessity of competition.[29]

The theory of surplus value (minus some of the qualifications and distinctions with which Marx hedged his discussion of it) has played a powerful role in the formation of revolutionary consciousness. That role has been to provide a similitude of scientific demonstration that the capitalist, as capitalist, robs the worker by extorting from him unpaid labor time, and that the rapacity of this extortion is an essential, not an accidental, feature of capitalist production.

Much criticism has been devoted to the "transformation problem" in Marx—the technical difficulty or perhaps impossibility of transforming labor values into relative prices. But those searching for root causes of exploitation in contemporary societies will not find this the most serious weakness in the surplus-value theory. Its most serious weakness, rather, lies in its contention that only current labor really produces value, and that the value "produced" by variable capital is extorted from current labor via the exchange mechanism. It is perfectly true that without the application of current labor, stored-up labor (capital) is sterile, but this is a mere commonplace. In certain forms (e.g., durable commodities) it may *acquire* value as a result of demand, but cannot *produce* new value by itself. The theory's fallacy is its failure to concede (or at least to recognize the full implications of the fact) that constant capital tremendously enhances the value-producing power of current labor.[30] Without it, current labor would be very nearly sterile. If people had not stored up labor by refraining from immediate gratification but instead using (and often risking) their wages to increase wealth, capital (whether constant or variable) would not exist. That portion of the value of commodities yielded to capital as interest would not exist, either.[31]

Marx claimed implicitly that stored-up labor, unlike present labor, deserves no return. His main line of argument depends upon the notion that it creates no value but simply absorbs it. This contention we have seen to be fallacious. There is, however, another and less prominent consideration that shaped his thinking on the subject: Capital was viewed by him, *even in its initial formation*, less as the stored-up product of the owner's own labor than as part of the expropriated product of the labor of others.[32] To the extent that he was partially correct in this, the expropriation, as he himself indicates, may be laid mainly at the door of the landlord, not of the capitalist.[33]

Profits from earnings of capital, or stored-up labor, are classified as interest. But profits may also include earnings or returns to another kind of labor, entrepreneurship. Without this kind of labor, which requires a scarce combination of traits and skills, the production of wealth would be diminished manyfold.

To Marx, however, entrepreneurship represents nothing other than capital as an active function, as distinct from capital as inert property. Since he held that the active function of capital is to exploit productive labor, the labor performed by the entrepreneur (whether he operates with borrowed capital or with his own) is simply that of an exploiter of the labor of others.

> The wage which he claims and pockets for this labour is exactly equal to the appropriated quantity of another's labour and depends directly upon the rate of exploitation of this labour, in so far as he undertakes the effort required for exploitation; it does not, however, depend on the degree of exertion that exploitation demands, and which he can shift to a manager for moderate pay.[34]

He is not an inventor, but an exploiter of the inventions of others.[35] As we have seen, he is not even necessarily a manager.

Marx fails to apprehend that neither invention nor management suffice to release the latent wealth-producing capabilities of "ordinary" labor. Ancient Greece had its inventors, but their inventions remained intellectual toys. Ancient Egypt had its managers, but their most renowned achievement was to superintend the building of sarcophagi. History attests that material abundance, in the last analysis qualitatively as well as quantitatively, rests upon the robust production and distribution of the *commodities* so despised by Marx. This requires the energetic vision that only entrepreneurship can provide.

Which is by no means to deny that among the ranks of professed "entrepreneurs" an inordinate share of parasites and con men may be found. They are convenient grist for the mills of those who would caricature and defame free enterprise. But the opening of the Iron Curtain has revealed to all but the most closed-minded that parasites and con men flourish at least equally abundantly under socialism.

Struggle to Fit "Class Struggle" Doctrine to Reality

Obviously, economic classes exist, and there has often been conflict between them. Marx fit this phenomenon into the framework of dialectical materialism. He "demonstrated" that the existence of classes is linked to the historical development of various modes of production, and that the class struggle must inevitably lead to the dictatorship of the proletariat. He concluded that the latter will constitute a transition to the abolition of all classes and the emergence of a classless society.[36]

Without embracing dialectical materialism, Gutiérrez seems to accept Marx's notion that the proletariat has a pivotal role to play in the revolutionary movement toward a society without classes and without oppression, for he speaks of the proletariat as the "most clear-sighted segment" of the poor.[37] Yet in Latin America, the proletariat (a term explicitly reserved by Marx for industrial wage workers) is relatively affluent; it ranks in the top quarter of income earners.[38] The truly marginalized masses there, as in the Third World at large, are composed of tenant farmers and other agricultural laborers, on the one hand, and jobless or casually employed urban slum dwellers, on the other. Of these, the first group corresponds most closely to the peasantry, which Marx considered hopelessly passive and reactionary; the second, to the "lumpenproletariat," which he thought so degraded that it could generate only beggars, criminals, and "scabs."

On the basis of Marx's schema, Latin America has scarcely any poor whom he would have thought capable of revolutionary consciousness, whereas the proletariat, which he regarded as alone capable of such consciousness, is not, in that geographical context, poor. (This remains true despite the fact that the lot of urban workers during the 1980s worsened in Mexico, Brazil, and other parts of Latin America, primarily as a result of inflation.) Insofar as liberation theologians have relied on Marxist analysis, what then becomes of their "preferential option for the poor"? Since Gutiérrez and his fellow liberationists, North and South, make it abundantly plain that by this preferential option they do not mean alleviating the misery of the poor in any paternalistic fashion, but rather through actively expressing solidarity with them in their fight for liberation, the Marxist version of who the classes are and what their roles are supposed to be can only lead to bewilderment.

This merely scratches the surface of why the doctrine of class struggle is a false compass. A deeper reason that the doctrine confuses the search for a way out of the Wasteland is the epistemology inherent in it. Specifically, under Marx's concept of logic as a class function, each class has its distinctive thought patterns that reflect its material interests. Truth is not to be discovered objectively "from the outside," but only through active commitment to working-class interests.

Latin American liberationists adopt this approach (and depart from European radical theologies such as those of Metz and Moltmann) to the extent they say theology must grow out of the revolutionary practices of the marginalized and exploited masses. For Marx, what gives special epistemic status to the proletariat is his belief that its class interests and class logic pave the way for the culmination of the class struggle, for universal emancipation, and its own extinction as a class: It is "a class which is the dissolution of all classes, a sphere of society which has a universal character because its sufferings are universal, and which claims no *particular right* because the wrong committed against it is not a *particular wrong* but *wrong as such.*"[39] The problem is that all of this is sheer assertion, demonstrated neither rationally nor empirically. As we have observed, the proletariat in Latin America does not belong to the lower economic strata of society. In those regions of the world where it has attained power through revolution, its leadership comes to constitute a new privileged class.

But since liberation theologians have never claimed Marxist orthodoxy, let us substitute the poor for the proletariat. There is doubtless a great deal to be learned from them, and, as Gutiérrez and Sobrino remind us, it cannot be learned through patronizing condescension.[40] To help the poor liberate themselves, we must understand their perspective, and to do this we must enter into their world, at least imaginatively if not by actually becoming poor ourselves. Yet the poor do not reflect a single outlook. Fortitude, humility, faith, and dignity are to be found among them. So, too, not surprisingly, are escapism, racism, chauvinism, pride in ignorance, and many other less-than-estimable attitudes. Sin cuts across class lines, even though its characteristic manifestations may tend to vary from class to class. The poor are not, any more than any other economic group, an exclusive or infallible repository of truth.

If perfect objectivity is impossible where class interests are concerned, this does not entitle us to throw up our hands and cease to strive for it. If impossible, it is what Reinhold Niebuhr calls "an impossible possibility."[41] Let us grant that Marx performed a service by calling attention to the extent to which class interests, frequently disguised, can warp our thinking. But as Christians, we are not permitted to assume that such warping is necessary or inevitable, for our faith bids us submit our partial and historically conditioned judgments to the arbitrament of an "ultimate ideal [that] always transcends every historical fact and reality."[42]

Does Socialism Liberate?

North Americans tend to be so confident that theirs is manifestly the best economic system (considering such problems as depressions, poverty, homelessness, and the like as aberrations) that they might view a critique by representatives of alternative systems as irrelevant.

Western observers were quick to declare a victory of capitalism over socialism during the collapse of a string of East European Marxist governments, often amid proclamations by rebel leaders of the need to establish free markets. Yet many of the same leaders warn against policies usually associated with capitalism that could induce joblessness and inflation. They seem to be seeking a vague middle ground that they themselves find difficult to define.

Lest free enterprisers be so smug about the present status of capitalism that they do not take seriously the reformers of less-capitalistic bent, turning the spotlight back on Latin America offers ample reasons for carefully addressing the outlook of those reformers and their followers.

Few if any Latin American experts would dispute Novak's finding that "capitalism, in the eyes of liberation theology, is the enemy."[43] Argentine Methodist liberationist José Míguez Bonino asserts that "the basic ethos of capitalism is definitely anti-Christian."[44] Kindred statements could be cited from the writings of Gutiérrez, Segundo, Assmann, Leonardo Boff, Miranda, Dussel, and others. McGovern perceptively remarked in 1989 that "while references to Marxism have become more muted and nuanced and the framework of liberation analysis has broadened, some use of Marxist analysis remains because it serves as the most prominent instrument of criticism against capitalism."[45] Gutiérrez is quoted in the *New York Times* as being "willing to entertain the idea that, if the evidence showed capitalism effectively relieving poverty, there could be a capitalist liberation theology"—but only as a very remote and highly theoretical possibility.[46]

What is this socialism, or the perception of it, that still has a strong hold on many people who are trying to overcome oppression by overturning "wicked" capitalism?

Describing the aims of the Paris Commune in 1871, Marx writes, "It wanted to make individual property a truth by transforming the means of production, land and capital, now chiefly the means of enslaving and exploiting labor, into mere instruments of free and associated labor," and, he declares, "this is Communism."[47]

What he designates as communism sounds surprisingly consistent with a free market and with the goals of genuine land reform. But the passage is far from an accurate portrayal of what Marx meant by communism:[48] the total abolition of the market.[49] How, in a modern economy, the market is to be prevented from reasserting itself is a point never explicitly addressed by Marx. The burden of proof now falls on his disciples to show that doing so does not require or lead to the police-state tactics of Josef Stalin and his ilk.

Marx's writings exhibit striking contrasts: severe realism when dealing with revolutionary strategy and romantic naïveté when posing his speculative ideal; voluminous complexity when offering his critique of capitalism, and fragmentary thinness when laying out his postrevolutionary program.

What happens after capitalism's supposedly inevitable overthrow? A proletarian dictatorship is to confiscate the means of production and abolish the exchange economy. Since the proletariat represents universal humanity, its rule will pave the way for a classless society and the disappearance of the state as an engine of class domination. Production will be for use and not for profit, but at first the product will be distributed (by means of noncirculating labor certificates)[50] in terms of the amount of socially useful labor each individual performs. In the "higher phase" of communist society, distribution determined by contribution will give way to the formula: "From each according to his ability, to each according to his needs!"[51]

Centralized planning in this millennium would banish waste by creating a perfect balance between supply and demand. It would orient technological development toward the well-being of the whole community. Planning and management, being, as Babeuf had put it, "a simple affair of numbering things and people,"[52] would require no special capacity or training, and would, like other types of mental or physical labor, presumably be shared by all members of the community through some system of rotation. In this way, the rounded development of persons would be assured. Directly associated production will revive the conviviality that marked human relations prior to commodity exchange, but now the full flowering of technological and organizational advance will engender comprehensive abundance. Individuals, no longer fettered by alienating privatism, will attain true liberation as their labor, instead of being externally imposed, wells forth in spontaneous expression of their authentic social nature.

Marx is not to be faulted for refraining from outlining, like Fourier, a blueprint so elaborately minute as to be ridiculous. Unknowable vicissitudes of time and place render detail premature beyond a certain point. Moreover, socialist faith in the ability of the proletariat to fashion its own concrete solutions once history has opened the way for it may be no more of a leap in the dark than is democratic faith in the collective wisdom of "the people."

Yet Marx might reasonably have been expected to do more than throw forth a few scattered hints about central planning and labor certificates in limning the "scientific" ordering of socialist society. How, for example, is technological advance to be sustained in a community of amateurs? On what are the planners to base their decisions as to allocation of material and human resources? How is central planning to be reconciled with (let alone make possible) Marx's freedom to shift from one occupation to another "just as I like," as often as several times a day? What is to prevent the initial dictatorship from petrifying into self-perpetuating oligarchy? Such questions should have demanded answers before thinking men and women committed themselves to revolution. With the hindsight of so many failed Marxist experiments, they certainly cannot now be avoided.

Papering over Dictatorship with Veneer of Humanism

Herbert Marcuse, guru of the New Left, responding to the demand that those who work for capitalism's replacement state concrete alternatives, departed (not uncharacteristically) from Marxist tradition to speculate as to the configuration of a regime of socialist humanism. Liberation theologians, by and large, have not been so bold in this respect. Yet since Marcuse's ideas have been a source of stimulation to them,[53] and since his neo-

Marxist humanism is in many ways congenial to their outlook, it is germane to review and comment on his speculations.

Marcuse visualizes "a revolution which subordinates the development of productive forces and higher standards of living to the requirements of creating solidarity for the human species, for abolishing poverty and misery beyond all national frontiers and spheres of interest, for the attainment of peace."[54] The rational use of advanced technology on a global scale would terminate poverty "within a very foreseeable future." But rational use and collective control would not by themselves ensure emancipation. A bureaucratic welfare state "would still be a state of repression which would continue even into the 'second phase of socialism,' when each is to receive 'according to his needs.'"[55] Collective control and planning of the means of production and distribution is the necessary foundation for liberation, but it is not enough.[56] "The new direction, the new institutions and relationships of production, must express the ascent of needs and satisfactions very different from and even antagonistic to those prevalent in the exploitative societies."[57] Human needs would no longer be geared to crass consumerism, to "spurious and parasitarian 'personalized' services . . . and the gadgets and tokens of exploitative affluence," but to "what can be reproduced and refined with a minimum of alienated labor."[58] All of this, including the reconstruction of human personality, is to be achieved without the prolongation of centralized authority since, "the anti-repressive sensibility, allergic to domination, would militate against" such prolongation.[59]

Although Marcuse calls his speculations "utopian," he holds that advanced technology has deprived utopia of its unreal content.[60] He implies that once demigods possessed of "the new sensibility" obtain power, they will create a people in their own image, a people whose instincts toward solidarity, tenderness, joy, and freedom would be released from the alienating fetters of commodity exchange. Then the apparatus of manipulation will be dismantled, and everyone will live happily ever after, world without end.

Gutiérrez, among the most temperate and balanced of the liberationists, remarks that despite the importance of Marcuse's ideas, "there are ambiguities, critical observations to be made, and points to be clarified."[61] That is putting it mildly.

Anticapitalism: Case of Mistaken Identity?

The anticapitalist bias of liberation theologians is not easy to untangle, because the system they harshly criticize is seldom recognizable as capitalism to North Americans or Europeans. Indeed, it is doubtful if it would have been recognized as such even by Marx, for whom free competition and legal (although not functional) equality were cardinal characteristics of capitalism, as he defined it. Arthur McGovern goes to the heart of the problem:

> The concentration of land ownership begun in colonial times contin-ues into the present with 1.3 percent of landowners in Latin America controlling 71.6 percent of all land under cultivation. This structure of concentrated ownership deprived the great masses of the popula-tion access to production; but one could also describe it in terms of the absence of any real experience of free enterprise.[62]

We do not dispute the oft-repeated claim that liberation theology is not mere theorizing but arises out of actual experience indigenous to specific contexts of oppression. In this framework it is scarcely plausible to assume that its Latin American articulators have expended time and effort oppos-ing something that scarcely exists in their milieu. This leaves no option but to conclude that they ingenuously apply the term *capitalism* to what is basically something else.

What is this something else? It is without doubt an oppressive order of privilege all too familiar in Latin America. It is heavily state-directed and dominated by a landowning elite — precisely the sort of social order attacked by the Physiocrats and Adam Smith, who first gave capitalism its theoretical underpinnings. Although this order has been widely characterized as feudal or quasi-feudal, Frank maintains that it was capitalist from the beginning.[63] However, he uses the word *capitalist* to signify what might be better termed "mercantilist."

The mere existence of private property and private profit do not define a system as capitalist, especially when that property and profit are tied to state-conferred monopoly. Capitalism is more properly understood as "a system of freely exchangeable private property rights in goods and services, with the central government protecting and enforcing these rights."[64] It involves open markets, equality before the law, and a disinclination toward public restriction of nonpredatory economic activity. It provides a frame-work for the individual pursuit of freely chosen values. Its thrust is toward the creation of new wealth rather than just the trading of commodities within an existing pool of wealth. This ideal does not obtain fully anywhere. But the point to be underscored is that the economic systems that obtain or ever have obtained in most of Central and South America have almost nothing in common with these basic tenets of capitalism.

To address the pejorative connotations that capitalism has acquired for many persons in many regions of the world, one must distinguish between the ideal, just stated, and actual practices. For example, when capitalism degenerates into a fixation upon private material aggrandizement, partic-ularly at the expense of ecological or other legitimately public concerns, it should be altered, not defended. Nor need anyone champion a capitalism that allows corruption and special privilege to gain the upper hand.

Fully worthy of defense, on the other hand, is the authentic core of capitalism, the free market. This should be upheld and championed primarily on moral and secondarily on social-utilitarian grounds. Freedom, we are convinced, is indivisible. The free market is nothing less than freedom in its economic aspect. The free market offers a wide latitude of economic options. It is perfectly compatible with producer or consumer cooperatives, with employee participation in both ownership and management, with non-profits and community-based credit mutuals, and so forth, as well as with more conventional commercial and industrial forms.

In the minds of many of its detractors, the free market is associated with imperialism. This is a serious misapprehension, although an understandable one to the degree that capitalist *nations* have pursued imperialist policies. Such pursuit has been strenuously decried by the most consistent free-market theoreticians—John Bright, Richard Cobden, Edwin L. Godkin, William Graham Sumner, Albert Jay Nock, Garet Garrett, and Murray Rothbard, to cite just a few. Instances of imperial behavior by the United States are doubly painful to the present authors because they undercut the guiding principles both of their country's economic system, capitalism, and its political system, representative government with constitutional safeguards against abuse of power.

A Feudal-Socialistic Stew

Does Latin America have a feudal economy? Like the feudal order, its status quo is marked by the presence of a largely hereditary landed oligopoly with strong military connections. But Frank is probably correct in claiming that it is not feudal, for under feudalism, hereditary status assumed a marriage between rights and obligations. The lord's right to his domain and to the service of his peasants was conditional upon his duty to protect "his" people. The peasant's obligation to give service was conditional upon his rights to the leasehold of his cottage, to free access to the commons, and to physical security. Of course, these preconditions were at times more honored in the breach than in the observance.

While not, strictly speaking, feudal, the status quo in Latin America is more socialist than capitalist. Banks and major corporations are often nationalized. Not uncommonly, a majority of the people receive the bulk of their income directly from the state. The tide now seems to have turned,[65] but at least as late as 1985, in Bolivia, an estimated 80 percent of employment was by the state, in Mexico, as much as 70 percent.[66] Prior to Paz Estenssoro's return to the presidency after the middle of that year, miserable, apathetic, inflation-ridden Bolivia, where virtually nothing flourished except the drug traffic, was probably the most thoroughly socialized nation in South America; according to one commentator, there was "almost nothing left to nationalize" there.[67]

Yet, having rejected what they understood to be capitalism, Latin American liberationists opt for socialism—not always of the Marxist brand, but socialism nonetheless. According to Segundo, "We give the name of socialism to a political regime in which the ownership of the means of production is removed from individuals and handed over to higher institutions whose concern is the common good."[68] But he declines to specify any means of assuring that these "higher institutions" would work for the common good rather than for the aggrandizement of state officials and their cohorts.

This is a problem with other liberation theologians as well. When asked to identify their closest existing concrete model, they demur, although many were emphatic in asserting before *glasnost* that the Soviet Union did not qualify.[69] Like Marx, while calling for absolute commitment to socialist revolution, they are short on specifics as to the institutional features of the program to be implemented, since "we cannot foresee or control the universe of the future."[70]

In seeking to justify this reticence, Segundo offers the following tortured analogy: When it is asked that Latin Americans "put forward a project for a socialist society which will guarantee in advance that the evident defects of known socialist systems will be avoided, why do we not demand of Christ also that before telling a sick man who has been cured, 'Your faith has saved you,' he should give a guarantee that that cure will not be followed by even graver illnesses?"[71] The Bible records no instance when Jesus promised permanent good health to anyone. His cures were always for particular illnesses and were performed in particular contexts. To compare them to a social elixir to be administered *en masse*, the ingredients of which are not precisely indicated, is to miss the mark. One might have expected better from an author whose work more typically displays great depth and richness.

To avoid the common error of comparing the unrealized ideal of one economic system with the actual working record of another, the empirical data from both socialist and capitalist nations should not be ignored. While no existing economic system fully embodies either the capitalist or the socialist model, many come close enough to provide reasonable bases for comparison. The United States, Canada, and Western Europe are acknowledged to be essentially capitalist. The most thoroughgoing examples of socialism are probably Albania, Kampuchea under Pol Pot, and mainland China during Mao Tse-tung's "Great Cultural Revolution." Are the latter superior to the former in their record of fostering freedom, community, and the flowering of human creativity?

We could say, of course, that the latter do not exemplify what liberation theologians mean by socialism. But no society that has ever existed does. Understanding is not advanced by opposing a vague, utopian, and unrealized ideal of socialism to the actual working of capitalism, which, however imperfect, is demonstrably far less oppressive as well as more successful in meeting economic needs than any form of actual socialism has ever been.

Basic Design Defects

Why have socialist nations, to overcome their dismal performance, often introduced capitalistic "impurities" — beginning as far back as Lenin's "New Economic Policy," with its reestablishment of some private farms and productivity incentives? Among the major reasons are the following.

Socialism's view of human nature as either naturally noble or almost totally malleable is fallacious. Many people do respond unselfishly when war or other crises call for sacrifice; but to expect them to act heroically to meet production quotas as a routine feature of day-to-day existence is unrealistic. To the extent that populations can be conditioned to behave that way, the price is to divest them of their humanity and to turn them into regiments of biped ants. Capitalism, for its part, without insisting that individuals are always animated by narrowly egoistic motives, does not depend upon lofty sentiments — whether natural or artificially conditioned — to operate effectively. An economic system is best grounded upon the assumption that people are generally self-centered, not upon the delusion that they are generally altruistic or the hope that environmental tinkering will make them so.

Archbishop Temple wisely observed that the art of government "is the art of so ordering life that self-interest prompts what justice demands."[72]

Socialism, whether totalitarian or democratic, is necessarily deficient in checks and balances. When the state is the sole employer, a worker has little recourse but to submit to state-imposed conditions of employment. The wage relationship, alleged to be such an alienating feature of capitalism, becomes under socialism an absolute tyranny within which there are few if any options, and beyond which there is essentially no appeal. Socialist workers thus yearn, not for the classless society, but for the right to choose from among many employers or self-employment, for the chance to shape their lives and pick their occupations as they wish — in short, for freedom.

The want of checks and balances is the ineluctable outcome of subjecting economics to politics. Concentrating all economic power in political hands assures formation of a *nomenklatura*, a new privileged class. Even if its members are not personally corrupt, there is little to limit their grandiosity. Under totalitarian socialism, this is obvious. Under democratic socialism, the abuse of power may be curbed by the necessity of facing the electorate. But because public budgets are not constrained by profit and loss statements, the appeal for votes is as likely to stimulate as to check grandiosity, giving rise to lavish programs funded through deficit spending and inflation.[73] "Is this the Promised Land?" asks a peasant couple approaching the border of the realm of Id. "It is during election year," comes the mordant answer.[74]

The pitfalls concerning grandiosity may be illustrated by reference to Brazil, Argentina, Mexico, and Peru. While not avowedly socialist, these nations all have public sectors of such magnitude in proportion to their total economies as to virtually insulate them from domestic market discipline. They stagger under the burden of enormous external debt. Their citizens resent even modest effort to retire the debt, for this usually means that exports must take precedence over production for domestic needs. (This is supposed, by dependency theorists, to demonstrate the domination of the center over the periphery.)

These crushing debts, it is maintained, were incurred by military rulers without any public mandate, and the borrowed funds often served to enrich corrupt officials and their cronies. This is partly but not altogether true. Mexico has not had a military government since 1914. Brazil's debt spiral began under an elected civilian president, Juscelino Kubitschek. A great deal of borrowed money did disappear into private pockets, but much was used for popular programs that improved general living standards in the short run, without any commensurate improvement in productive capacity to sustain them. Many experts fear that the austerity measures requisite for repaying the debts would topple any government that seriously tried to implement them. So the call is for rescheduling as the only alternative to default or repudiation.

Contrast South Korea, which, despite authoritarian military rule until perhaps recently, has an essentially market-oriented economy. Its obligations to foreign creditors were met promptly and without strain because the substantial sums borrowed were invested in ways that led to massive increase in gross national product instead of being spent directly to raise levels of consumption. As the benefits of economic growth spread throughout the population, the standard of living rose steadily.

Socialism, in the sense of a centrally planned ("command") economy, has no rational measure for determining costs and prices. This charge of pragmatic unworkability, first set forth in 1920 by von Mises, has never been convincingly rebutted.[75] Without the constant pulling and tugging of a free market to reveal what people want and will pay, decisions about what and how much to produce and what to charge must be made according to noneconomic, frequently political, criteria or sheer guesswork. In some spheres, national defense for example, it is unavoidable to make production decisions on the basis of noneconomic criteria; but it is precisely for this reason that military procurement is notoriously wasteful and extravagant.

What is an inherent but regrettable necessity in special cases under capitalism becomes, under socialism, typical of the entire economy. Socialist societies would be plagued even more severely by scarcity, waste, and distortion if they did not permit within their orbit some free markets and did not monitor pricing and production information from their capitalist competitors.

Following the lead of Oskar Lange, "market socialists" claim that central authorities can obtain supply and pricing information from such indicators as depletion rates of factory inventories. Managers at local levels would

then orient their production schedules to these data. This claim seems far-fetched and farcical. To gather and transmit back the necessary information quickly enough to adjust thousands of daily decisions to changing conditions would be a superhuman task. And mere statistics provide inadequate guidance: Does a factory have a glut of shoes because people already have plenty? Because these shoes are of poor quality or an unpopular design? Because of distribution breakdowns? If almost everyone at every stage in the production cycle had a financial stake, they would make it their business to find the answers. However, when wages, jobs, and business survival are not at stake, and when consumers cannot "vote" with their pocketbooks, meaningful signals do not filter up to the decision makers.

When prices are set by bureaucrats who undergo no personal risk, the process is a charade and the prices are fictitious. Such prices, that is, do not perform the many vital services that are so commonplace they are taken for granted in free market countries — helping to conserve scarce resources, killing unsatisfactory products, inducing the birth of new ones, and so forth.

One suspects that "market socialism" might long ago have been given up, in practice and in theory, as a poor counterfeit of the genuine free market, except for one big problem: *Many so-called free markets are not free.* Many capitalist economies permit monopolies, government interference, special privileges, and destructive land policies to undercut the virtues of a free market and to spawn critical social problems that have sullied the reputation of the free market.

Beyond Michael Novak

To recapitulate, liberation theology is an authentic spiritual movement animated by legitimate social concerns, but sometimes guided by questionable compasses, especially the theories of dependency, alienation, surplus value, class struggle, and socialism.

Several points that we have made in seeking to substantiate this perspective were taken, not always without change, from the works of Michael Novak, particularly from his book, *Will It Liberate?* Over the years, Novak has drawn the ire of many liberationists who have seen him as an apologist for North American capitalism. And it is true that in a 1984 *New York Times Magazine* article, Novak presented liberation theology as "fundamentally naive" and in danger of delivering South America into the hands of communism.[76] But, in *Will It Liberate?* (and elsewhere), Novak takes liberation theology seriously[77] and attempts to open a constructive dialogue with its exponents. In isolated passages, his zeal appears to lead him to distorted representations of liberationist views and to arguments that are less than cogent.[78] But on the whole we see his critique as apt, penetrating, and offered in a spirit of Christian collegiality and good faith.

Yet Novak is disappointing; not so much in what he says as in what he

fails to say. "With the liberation theologians," he asserts, "we may all agree that the social system of Latin America requires fundamental reordering, not simply reform."[79] Again and again he adverts to the primacy of the land question.[80] And he speaks of the need to use the taxing power to promote and maximize economic creativity rather than to repress it.[81] Yet nowhere does he advance any concrete suggestions as to how to address the land question. Nor does he offer any road maps for maximizing economic creativity through enlightened tax policy.

One might be inclined to attribute these lacunae to a North American's diffidence about prescribing policies to the peoples of another continent and culture. But Novak displays no diffidence in prescribing free markets, institutions to make credit readily available, the abolition of legal impediments to starting and operating businesses, the protection of property rights in inventions and literary works, and on and on.[82]

These are all worthy recommendations, deserving of adoption. But they do not touch the most basic and pervasive of all socioeconomic maladies in Latin America—the stripping of the people's land rights—or point the way to its remediation.[83]

8

Traveling Down the King's Highway

How Those in Power Maintain the Status Quo

After many years in the wilderness of Zin, Moses sent to the king of Edom messengers who, after recounting the liberation of his people from Egyptian bondage through the Lord's intervention, asked permission for the Hebrews to pass through the territory of Edom along the King's Highway en route to the Promised Land (Num. 20:14–21). The king refused, so the people skirted Edom and journeyed on to the Negeb. There they were opposed by the king of Arad, who fought them. After utterly obliterating the king and his army, they arrived eventually at the boundary of the Amorites. They then petitioned Sihon, the Amorite ruler, trying once more to go by the King's Highway. Sihon refused and battled against Israel in the wilderness. As with Arad, Sihon and his men were destroyed (Num. 21:21–24). After that, Og, king of Bashan, fought Israel, and he too was killed (Num. 21:33–35).

Let this be an allegory for oppressed people in the last decade of the twentieth century. The King's Highway is a pathway that leads out of the Wasteland to the Promised Land. Controlling the highway are opponents of justice who wish to confine the people to the wilderness, to misery. These little "kings" marshal all of their forces to prevent the people from getting through to their land. So consumed are they with opposition to a righteous social order that they usurp the highway to social equity, thus risking the destruction of their nations and themselves.

Clearing Away Roadblocks

To journey down the King's Highway to a realm where all people have equal opportunity, freedom, and access to the land, it is necessary to clear away some intellectual roadblocks erected by those who seek to keep the land as their exclusive personal preserve. These mental roadblocks to progress are often more insidious than they seem, because they become adopted as truths, not only by the exploiters, but by their oppressed victims as well.

Some old means of inducing complacency and acceptance of widespread involuntary poverty can be sidestepped just by mentioning them, such as shifting blame to the sins of ancestors, to misdeeds in previous incarnations and—ultimate blasphemy—to the will of God.

Two other rationalizations, the wages fund theory and Malthusianism, require a closer look, because these nineteenth-century ideas, appearing now in new clothing, have been appropriated by the rich and powerful to justify the status quo.

Which Comes First—Capital or Labor?

According to the wages fund theory, labor is employed by capital. Wages, limited by available capital, must be kept low to avoid large-scale unemployment. To put it another way, low wages make it possible to accumulate more capital, which in turn assures fuller employment. Like most erroneous theories, this one rests upon some valid insights. Capital does enhance labor's power to create wealth. Excessive wages can retard the upkeep, replacement, and expansion of capital; if production slows, real wages can decrease, and jobs may be lost. But the basic theory is fallacious.

Labor employs capital, not the reverse. Otherwise, how would capital come into existence? Labor made the original tools, and again employed these to make more capital. In modern production, wages are normally paid out of the wealth labor itself is creating. These wages reflect an increase in the capital stock due to the labor for which they are paid, not a diminution of some preexisting "wages fund."

A paucity of capital is not, as international development banks, foreign aid programs, and even Third World development advocates typically profess, a basic reason for poverty. The most wretched and degrading poverty is usually found in great urban centers, such as Calcutta or Mexico City, where capital is abundant. Production flourishes in such places, but the mass of people get no fair share of the wealth they help produce; in economic terms, distribution is seriously flawed and much of labor's earnings are expropriated.

Introducing more capital to produce still more wealth, as panegyrists of development continuously propose, is no solution. But neither is simply redistributing existing wealth, as socialists or welfare-state proponents urge, for that stifles initiative and shrinks the "pie" to be divided. Neither of these wage-fund approaches will suffice. Rather, snuffing out poverty calls for instituting equitable distribution of *current* production, thus providing dynamic incentives to labor and capital alike. In Latin America, such incentives rarely exist, or ever have. Where opportunities for enterprise are not choked by monopoly or bureaucratic interference, the wealth created is too often siphoned off by elements that contribute little if anything to the productive process.

Does Increased Population Mean More Poverty?

Scarcely anyone today accepts Malthus's formula that population increases geometrically while food supply increases arithmetically, so that only vice, famine, pestilence, and war are keeping the human species from outrunning the bounds of subsistence by holding their numbers in check.[1]

Yet Malthusianism, in the sense of the general notion that poverty is chiefly the result of overpopulation, has undergone striking revival, as evidenced by the gloomy prognostications of the Club of Rome.[2] Reforms to better the health and life-expectancy of the poor are seen as self-defeating, for they simply encourage reckless propagation. Nothing but compulsory birth control combined with strict conservation of nonreproducible natural resources can stave off the exhaustion of nature's gifts and the resultant doom of humankind.

While neo-Malthusianism too is grounded on valid insights, obvious counter-illustrations come to mind. Japan and Holland are among the world's most densely populated nations and are poorly endowed with natural resources. If poverty were primarily due to overpopulation, their standards of living would be extremely low. The very opposite is true. Also, recent advances suggest that agricultural technology has barely scratched the surface in boosting the world's potential ability to raise food.

There may be a point at which the earth's population could outstrip its means of subsistence, but that point is far from being reached. None of what has been said, we hasten to emphasize, should be taken as an argument against family planning or conservation, both of which can and should be defended on other grounds.

Our position is simply this: Overpopulation is not the major cause of world poverty; it does not offer a valid excuse for its continuance; and it does not hold the key to its cure.

Several phenomena give neo-Malthusianism superficial plausibility. For one, Third World production of wealth has not kept pace with growing population. For another, such production that has occurred is often ecologically detrimental. But the most critical factor which leads inadvertently to concern about population numbers is *maldistribution*. This typically takes two forms.

Major shares of wealth are diverted to privileged interests that do nothing to create this wealth; this leaves large segments of society in miserable want, deprived of their fair shares.

In order to ward off revolt due to this maldistribution and to buy a semblance of social calm, part of the wealth is channeled back to the wretched masses — as "bread and circuses," subsidies of various kinds, palliatives, frequently to the tune of administrative favoritism and corruption. The tragedy of these public doles to the poor is that they bolster the status quo, perpetuating instead of disturbing the patterns of maldistribution that cause the problem. So they block the march to justice.

Seeking Poverty's Root Cause

Having dealt with certain roadblocks, let us reenter the King's Highway to seek the root cause of poverty. What initial maldistribution of wealth rewards parasites at the expense of workers? From whichever direction the question is approached, the signs all point to one great inescapable phenomenon: the stranglehold of the landowners over the landless.

Many people are diverted from grasping that inequitable land arrangements are a fundamental — in our view, *the* fundamental — cause of poverty because of the common habit of associating *land* only with agriculture and rural life. Because society is increasingly urban and industrial, this outlook makes land seem a quaint concern from a bygone past.

Land looms much much larger than that. *All* human existence still rests on the land. Urban poverty is not only exacerbated by the influx of landless paupers from the countryside. It arises directly from maldistribution and overconcentration of land rights *within* cities. City people no less than farmers live and work on land. Their homes, offices, and factories are constructed from products of the land. Their clothing, food, and cars, their heat and light, their newspapers and TVs — virtually every material item they can feel and touch — all have their origins in something grown on the land or in some substance taken from the land.

In the countryside, if people are starving while they are being fenced out of unused fertile land from which they could feed themselves, the land access problem is obvious. In the city, vacant lots represent potential shelter that is being denied to the homeless and potential jobs being denied to the unemployed. But for some reason, this urban land access problem has not been so obvious to antipoverty advocates. It would seem that, as men and women moved away from immediate contact with the soil, they became desensitized to their utter dependence on the land.

Other forms of exploitation besides denial of the birthright to land play a role in pervasive poverty, but they tend to be of a secondary nature. Take "wage slavery," to which poverty is popularly linked. Fair access to land gives labor strong bargaining power: Employers must offer as much in wages as self-employed workers can earn on readily available sites. Thus miserly wages are not a prime cause of deprivation so much as a symptom of labor's subjection to monopolistic land policies that force workers to take whatever pay is offered.

Defining Terms in Pursuit of Essential Relationships

Many liberation theologians do not even include the term *land* in the indexes of their books. This is not to point fingers at them; they are following, on the one hand, the papal encyclicals *Mater et Magistra* and *Populorum Progressio* that were less concerned with land than with the economic effects of labor unions, multinational corporations, neocolonialism, socialism, and capitalism,[3] and, on the other, certain economists whose sloppy terminology has helped to camouflage the critical role of landownership. As a corrective, we must get back to basics and pay attention to some key economic definitions and relationships.

Land refers to the whole material universe, exclusive of man and his products. It is not the creation of human labor, but it is essential to labor, for it is the raw material from which all wealth is fashioned. Unlike produced commodities, its supply cannot be increased to meet demand. Land includes not just the soil, but also water, minerals, wildlife, natural vegetation. It subsumes the idea of space or location as well as of matter. It is the passive factor in production, yielding wealth only when labor is applied to it.

Labor includes all human powers, mental or physical, used directly or indirectly to produce goods or to render service in exchange. A dynamic factor in production, it includes entrepreneurship and superintendence.

Wealth signifies tangible things that result from the application of labor to land and satisfy human wants. Because these things that satisfy wants have a degree of scarcity, they possess exchange value. Money, bonds, and mortgages are not wealth, as commonly expressed; they merely represent wealth, actual things whose ownership they symbolize; or they measure the value for which that wealth may be traded.

Capital is wealth which, instead of being consumed, is used to aid in further production of wealth. Since production is not completed until the product reaches the ultimate consumer, capital is sometimes defined as "wealth in the course of exchange" — exchange being understood to include transportation and merchandising. Capital, like labor, is a dynamic factor in production.

Just as these three factors — land, labor, and capital — define all production, the total sum of wealth they produce is distributed back among the three factors. The share to land is called *rent*; to labor, *wages*; to capital, *interest*. Properly used, these terms mutually exclude one another. Payments that are not returns to these factors, such as taxes, are drawn either from rent, wages, interest, or some combination of them.

Rent is wealth received by the owner of land by virtue of ownership, irrespective of any improvement on it or work performed on it. It accrues to an owner in payment for letting others use it. If an owner uses the land, rent is what he would have to pay for it, were he not the owner. The selling value of land is rent capitalized (what you would have to invest, say, in a bank to get a cash flow equal to the annual rent).[4]

Wages is the wealth labor gets for its contribution to the production of goods or services. Salaries, fees, and commissions are all included under this term. Those who work for themselves—businessmen, professionals, independent farmers—also receive wages, defined as that portion of their income attributable to their labor.

Interest is the share received by an owner of capital for making that capital available. If a producer uses his own capital, that part of his income attributable to its use is interest. Money on loan earns income that is commonly called "interest," based on a current "interest rate," but is it interest in the economic sense? Yes, if the loan is used entirely for producing wealth. If used for buying land, the return on it is rent. If used to purchase consumer goods, the return is wages—paid out of the borrowers' past or future earnings.[5] Interest is a premium for abstaining from consumption of wealth in order that it may be put to productive use. It is not, as is frequently said, compensation for risk because "the higher returns to capital engaged in risky enterprises are intended to take care of losses and in the long run bring the average return to the ordinary rate."[6]

The definitions[7] equip one to engage in the more revealing and meaningful analysis of the dynamics of production, including the central issue of how wealth is, or should be, distributed to the three factors of production.

A key to unravelling the puzzle is a nineteenth-century formulation known as Ricardo's *law of rent*. It is still generally accepted, although certain phenomena in some places may mitigate the full force of its operation. First stated in terms of agricultural land, its pertinence to *all* land is so patent as to require no demonstration. Where strenuous efforts to offset the impact of the law of rent have been undertaken in the Third World, the price has almost invariably been crippling inflation and external debt. The law reads: *The rent of land is determined by the excess of its produce over that which the same application can secure from the least productive land in use.*

The "produce" refers to the actual or potential wealth generated when a given site is put to optimum use—agricultural, extractive, manufacturing, commerce, residential, or whatever. "Application" refers to the utilization of labor and capital on that site. The "least productive land in use" means the best available free land, referred to as marginal land or the margin of production.

I may have very rich land, but it will yield no rent and have no value so long as there is other land as good to be had without cost. But when this other land is appropriated, and the best land to be had for nothing is inferior, either in fertility, situation, or some other quality, my land will begin to have a value and yield rent. . . . Rent, in short, is the price of monopoly, arising from the reduction to individual ownership of natural elements which human exertion can neither produce nor increase.[8]

An inevitable corollary of the law of rent is that wages and interest on any given site above the margin cannot together exceed the produce at the margin, for the difference will be absorbed by rent. As population increases, the margin is inexorably pushed out to poorer and poorer lands. Meanwhile, gains in productivity, development, and the growth of income (translated into effective demand) all tend to raise the value of land. (In the language of contemporary factoral income distribution theory, economic development shifts the schedule of the marginal value productivity of land to the right. Growth in population and income strengthens demands for the output of land, while the accumulation of factors complementary with land augments its marginal productivity, even in a physical sense.) The owner of land, in the long run, reaps the bulk of these advantages, so less remains for capital and labor.

From Urban Blight to Rain Forest Destruction — Bitter Fruits of Land Speculation

Speculative withholding of land exacerbates this process, pushing the margin prematurely out to even poorer lands. In urban centers it blocks downtown expansion, causes buildings to fall into disrepair, and turns neighborhoods into slums. It prevents developers from acquiring close-in plots at feasible prices, forcing them to the outskirts, where land is relatively cheap. The resulting "sprawl" engulfs farms and forests and wastes public funds by adding pressure for duplicating and extending schools, roads, sewers, and other public works and services that remain underused in the cities and close-in suburbs. It also drives up the price of rural acreage, making farming and suburban development more costly.

At times speculative withholding may prevent a site's premature development. More often it artificially induces the premature development of other land. Speculation is sometimes justified by claiming it allocates land to its proper uses. But this function would be performed even if landowners were deprived of the incentive to speculate. Entrepreneurs would still have the same incentives to find the most appropriate locations for development. Motivation for responsible land use requires *security of tenure*; it does not rely on the privilege of appropriating land rent, or even on the ownership of land. To accept this should present no difficulty to anyone who realizes how many major developments — Rockefeller Center, the Waldorf Astoria Hotel, and the Chrysler Building, to name a few in New York City — have been constructed on leased land.

Withholding land from use, typically induced by anticipation of speculative profit, has egregious manifestations other than those we have already mentioned, such as blocking society's use of regions with prime potential for agriculture, mineral extraction, recreational enjoyment, and other important purposes.

Rapid destruction of the Amazon rain forest in Brazil dramatizes how unnaturally extending the margin has an ominous worldwide impact on the environment. According to a recent government report, *Brasil 2000*, 10 percent of the landowners in this vast nation own 80 percent of the land, while 1 million peasants are forced off the land each year. A mere 1 percent controls 48 percent of the cultivable land.[9]

> The only place in Brazil where there is land for the taking is in the rain forest of the huge Amazon basin. Since 1970, 5 to 10 million people have migrated to this northern frontier. . . .
>
> Conservative estimates suggest an area of Amazon forest the size of Connecticut is cut and burned every year. But the region's fragile topsoil cannot sustain cultivation for long. Because the land degrades into useless brush a few years after it is cleared, the migrants push ever further into the forest in search of land that can support them.
>
> The Amazon basin is a critical link in the global ecosystem. It holds a quarter of the world's tropical rainforest and a greater diversity of living creatures than any area on earth. As many as two million species can be found there, but as the forest goes, the habitat of thousands of those species is lost. The forests are also a vital buffer against the global greenhouse effect because they absorb carbon dioxide that would otherwise trap the sun's heat.[10]

Without this buffer, the planet faces the prospect of massive crop-destroying drought and the melting of the polar icecaps, causing oceans to rise and low-lying coastal areas to become inundated. The rain forest would not be succumbing to these assaults if the present system did not perpetuate artificial land shortages. Nearly four-fifths of Brazil's arable acreage is covered by sprawling *latifundios*, half of which are held by speculators who produce nothing.[11]

Pushed to the Margin

Here is the connection with poverty. When the margin of production is pushed to land that can barely maintain life, labor itself is marginalized and must compete on this level. Wages generally, on all land, are driven down toward this point of bare subsistence. Returns to capital are also depressed for the same reason, deterring investment. When this is carried to an extreme — when people can no longer afford the goods being produced and when there is little profit in applying capital — the economy collapses.

The inflated land market, on which the speculative frenzy has fed, collapses too.

Since the Great Depression, such total economic ruin has been somewhat minimized in the more developed nations through Keynesian measures. Monetary expansion, massive public works and welfare programs cushion the full impact of destructive land policies. These expedients do not touch the root cause of poverty and recessions. Rather, they shore up a rotten structure, preventing disagreeable natural correctives or genuine reforms from coming into play.

In the Third World, where the prevalence of land monopoly has almost always kept the margin close to the point of bare subsistence, such Keynesian expedients purchase temporary relief and support high speculative rent levels. Band-Aid approaches may be sustainable if demand for exports is strong, but when that demand weakens, the toll is a weight of external debt so crushing as to defy redemption.

Ethical Basis of Ownership

If poverty is preeminently a problem of landownership, it becomes imperative to examine the moral basis of ownership. What gives us the right to own anything? And how does this apply to land?

The right of ownership does not come out of thin air but rests on our faith that human beings have been created as free moral agents, called to glorify their Creator through voluntary obedience to his will. To function as such, an individual must have a right to his or her person and to his or her labor, which is an extension of this person—the self expended, with varying degrees of intensity, in time. The exercise of this right includes the right to consume, exchange, give away, or simply keep what you produce. This right obtains against all other human beings, limited only by acts that interfere with the rights of others to what they produce.

It is on this account that theft is wrong; it constitutes a sort of partial murder—the taking of someone's crystallized past life. It is on this account that mankind finally came around to consider slavery wrong, as an unconscionable total theft of someone's labor.

Ownership is thus justified by labor. This concept, associated with the name of John Locke, was prefigured by Paul's comments on Moses' prohibition against muzzling an ox when it is treading out grain (Deut. 25:4). As the ox has a right to a share in this grain, a human being must have a right to the fruits of his labor (1 Cor. 9:7–10).

Are there other justifications for ownership? "Conquest," or might makes right, is beneath the consideration of those concerned with ethics. "Social utility" is too vague and slippery, leaving room for those who choose to practice theft or slavery in the name of the general good. "Need" as a basis for ownership, aside from being unduly subject to interpretation, founders on the shoal of what Christian doctrine terms "Original Sin," for there is no logical reason to assume that the mere needs of sinners give them rights.[12] It would thus appear that for the Christian, labor can be the *only* justification for ownership.[13] The labor argument, as adumbrated here, is not an argument from natural rights in the rationalistic eighteenth-century sense, but from what Lord Acton eloquently spoke of as "the equal right of every man to be unhindered in the fulfillment by man of duty to God — a doctrine laden with storm and havoc, which is the secret essence of the Rights of Man."[14]

Who Made and Owns the Land?

If human labor is the test, land, as previously defined, cannot be owned in the sense of belonging exclusively to particular persons, for land clearly is not a product of human labor. Of God's labor, yes. It was created before mankind as a storehouse of natural opportunity. Human labor cannot operate without it. Just as you cannot be a free moral agent "unhindered in the fulfillment by man of duty to God" if you are denied the full ownership of your own labor, neither can you play that role if you are denied fair access to land — the space and raw materials that are absolute prerequisites for all production and survival itself.

Locke affirmed that "God gave the world to men in common."[15] But he held that the mixing of labor with land through cultivation and the like may establish a kind of equity in it, just as the mixing of labor with land in the production of goods establishes an equity in them. While he was thus willing to countenance private ownership of land, he added a condition sometimes called the "Lockean Proviso," to wit, that there be "enough, and as good left in common for others."[16] In economic terms, this means so long as land has no market value. Writing at a time when vast fertile regions of the world remained practically unsettled, Locke may not have grasped the full implications of his own proviso. It would have precluded, even then, the ownership of any land above the margin, because "as good" implies not merely natural richness but also convenience of location, and would have disallowed plundering of natural resources in a manner that did not benefit "men in common." When one mixes one's labor with land so as to abstract scarce or potentially scarce natural resources from the common store, justice requires that arrangement be made for their replenishment or, if this cannot be done, that some equivalent be placed in trust as an indemnity to later generations.

The ownership of land, insofar as it shuts people off from access to nature's opportunity, save on the owner's terms, is tantamount to the ownership of people. "Place one hundred men on an island from which there is no escape, and whether you make one of these men the absolute owner of the other ninety-nine, or the absolute owner of the soil of the island, will make no difference either to him or to them."[17]

While this may seem an extreme example, it is sadly not far removed from actual situations in many places in the Third World. Elsewhere, where landownership is distributed more evenly, the monopoly effect is attenuated. But since people's survival depends on the use of land, so long as they must pay *anything* for the use of it to landlords who did nothing to create it, they are to that extent subjugated by the landlords.

In common usage, "landlord" often refers not only to the owner of land, but also to the owner of a house or building on the land. Clearly these structures are man-made, and those who produce and maintain them are entitled without question to a just reward. Adding to the confusion, the reward to building owners is commonly called rent. In economics (refer to the earlier definitions), the buildings are "capital" and the payment of those who make use of this capital for shelter or commerce is more properly termed "interest."

At issue in this discussion is ownership of land as such and the rent that arises due to natural or societal characteristics. That some people may be landlords in both senses does not obliterate these substantial distinctions based on the logic and ethics of the wealth-creating process.

In view of the justification of ownership by labor, it is ironic that title to land, the one material good which human labor did not create, is usually held in perpetuity, whereas title to literary, artistic, or musical compositions, which come as close as anything to being *pure* creations of human labor, is recognized by law only for a limited period of time.

Finders Keepers?

Here are arresting comments on the legitimacy of land titles:

Does the first passenger who enters a railroad car obtain the right to scatter his baggage over all the seats and compel the passengers who came in after him to stand up? ... We arrive and we depart, . . . passengers from station to station, on an orb that whirls through space — our rights to take and possess cannot be exclusive; they must be bounded everywhere by the equal rights of others. Just as the passenger in a railroad car may spread himself and his baggage over as many seats as he pleases, until other passengers come in, so may a settler take and use as much land as he chooses, until it is needed by others — a fact which is shown by the land acquiring a value — when his right must be curtailed by the equal rights of others, and no priority of occupation can give a right which will bar these equal rights of others. If this were not the case, then by priority of appropriation one man could acquire and transmit to whom he pleased ... a whole continent.[18]

The hardy pioneer who is the first to occupy and tame a portion of the wilderness indeed possesses a moral right to the fruits of his toil. Yet this scarcely conveys to him or his descendants a moral right to anything but that portion's products and improvements. Why should the fact that he arrived first authorize him to deny to later pioneers, or to members of future generations, a place where they may toil, or dictate terms on which that toil may be exercised? Claims based on first occupancy, or on "occupancy and use," are further flawed by ambiguity and imprecision. What determines the spacial limits of just occupancy? How, specifically, is "use" to be defined?

Some defenders of the status quo concede that all land titles may be traced either to acts of fraud or force or to the more respectable priority of occupation. Further, they admit that justice — *if* we could start from scratch — might well demand a social order that disallowed private property in land. But they protest this is not our situation. These same critics of land tenure reform insist we have to deal with "facts as they exist," not with some hypothetical state of affairs. The facts they stress are that society has for centuries given legal sanction to private landed property; that innumerable contracts have been executed on the basis of that sanction; and that these include the good faith purchase of land with wages and interest. For society to now invalidate land titles would not only be a breach of trust, it would also nullify the rewards of labor for those who, in all innocence, acquired land by exchanging hard-earned wages or interest for it, or who bequeathed land so acquired to their descendants.

Those who argue in this fashion overlook some other pertinent "facts as they exist."

No nation or community ever had a legitimate right to grant to private parties absolute title to something created by nature for the use and benefit of all. This concept is dimly and imperfectly reflected in the principle of eminent domain. No king ever had a moral right to legalize the spoil of conquered land. No legislature ever had a moral right to grant away the patrimony of a nation. No court ever had a moral right to vest perpetually in any family that which was intended for the people as a whole. So much for origins.

Do Old Wrongs Become Rights?

Moreover, the passage of time cannot turn a wrong into a right. The natural heritage of the race is inalienable, no less than other human rights, so years of contracts and titles cannot invalidate every person's equal claim to the land. "Because I was robbed yesterday, and the day before, and the day before that, is it any reason that I should suffer myself to be robbed today and tomorrow? Any reason that I should conclude that the robber has acquired a vested right to rob me?"[19]

Land bought with the proceeds of honest labor may be likened to a stolen watch purchased by some unsuspecting person in good faith. Neither the innocence of the purchaser nor his honestly gained money generates clear title to the stolen watch. A lesson of the United States' Civil War has been lost if people suppose society's recognition of a legal title takes precedence over ethics. This society once recognized legal titles to slaves, some of whom were no doubt purchased with honest money. Such considerations cannot justify practices and institutions that are essentially immoral.

If acquisition of a benefit under the law established a vested right to it in perpetuity, no law could ever be amended, since any change in law invariably works to someone's disadvantage. Reform of any kind would be impossible.

All in all, this pursuit of correct economic relationships makes a serious indictment of land tenure institutions in almost every nation. If this is where we are led in the search for the Promised Land—for insights into the causes and cures of the world's sickness with poverty—we do not flinch from it.

But what we have said affords no brief for precipitate and drastic changes that bring widespread ruin in their wake, even where abstract justice might support them. Changes that rend the fabric of society are almost always self-defeating. Oppressive structures ought, of course, to be dismantled. As to beneficiaries of those structures, the vast majority are not intentional wrongdoers but merely passive recipients of unearned increments from a flawed system they did not create, so the dismantling should be done in ways that avoid excessive hardship for them.

"Little kings" who go out of their way to oppose the march toward justice are in a different category. Where they block the Highway of the King of Kings, seeking through subterfuge and violence to maintain control, their arrogance invites no mercy. Yet our concern and focus is not with them, as individuals, but on the institutions or structures upon which their unjust power is based.

9

Claiming the Promised Land

Biblical Guideposts to Twentieth-Century Land Reform

The Bible is beloved variously as word of God, history, poetry, and more. Certain biblical passages will now be reviewed in careful detail, not as allegories, but to uncover economic insights that are remarkably relevant for understanding and healing poverty and oppression in all corners of our world—justifying still further respect and reverence for this great treasure.

After wandering in the wilderness, the people of Israel finally entered into the Promised Land. According to the account in Joshua, priests carrying the ark of the covenant stepped into the Jordan, which miraculously dried up, allowing the people to cross over (Josh. 3). Representatives from the twelve tribes then took stones from the riverbed and set up a marker in Gilgal as a reminder of God's leadership (Josh. 4:19–24). While the Hebrews were encamped there, they celebrated the Passover. A sense of the religious pervades the scene (Josh. 5:11).

We are struck by what follows in the book of Joshua. Even though God had willed the land to Israel, the tribes still had to engage painstakingly in wars to take possession of it.[1] This seems as true today as it was three thousand years ago: The Promised Land is a gift from God, but a gift that has to be claimed. What follows aims to suggest a way to claim the Promised Land for our time.

Moses' Unique Laws to Assure Freedom and Equality

To claim the land effectively, something beyond taking possession was required. Even before the actual conquest, the Law prescribed a method whereby that possession was to be rendered pleasing in God's sight. The Canaanites' claim, in contrast, was forfeited by their idolatry, with human sacrifice and temple prostitution, and by their exploitive, monopolistic social order. To make good *its* claim, Israel had to institute a social order that would guard against the desecration, pollution, and injustices of which its predecessors were guilty.

The Mosaic prohibitions against idolatry are familiar. Less familiar but more directly relevant to our theme are the Mosaic provisions for social justice — *for securing to each family and to every generation* within the Hebrew commonwealth *the equal right to the use of the land*, of which the Lord was recognized as the sole absolute owner.

These provisions, devised for primitive agrarian communities, included the germ of a principle applicable to complex industrial and mercantile societies. They began with a census of the tribes and families, taken on the plains of Moab prior to the conquest (Num. 26:1–51). A body consisting of one member from each tribe, jointly headed by Joshua and the priest, Eleazar, was charged with the duty of dividing the land. Every tribe — Levi excepted — and, within these tribes each family, was to receive its proportionate share, depending on its size (Num. 26:55–56). To insure the fairness of this division, the final apportionment was to be by lot (Num. 34:16–29).

The actual distribution of land in keeping with these provisions was concluded at Shiloh (Josh. 19:51). According to Josephus, the territory was not divided into shares of equal *size*, but rather into shares of equal agricultural *value*.[2] "The boundaries of the family allotments were carefully marked, and the sanctity of these 'landmarks' — the outward and visible signs of the equal right to the use of the earth — was protected by the public and solemn denunciation of a curse against him who should dishonestly tamper with them (Deut. 27:11–16; 19:14)."[3]

The Jubilee and a Sabbath for the Land

As land distribution reformers in our century have discovered, it is easier to devise a one-time apportionment that is fair than to keep the system from falling apart.

This is why the ancient Law established the Jubilee Year.[4] It assured that the equal rights of every family to the use of the land would be conserved from generation to generation. At the end of every fifty years, any alienated lands — those given away, sold, or lost from unpaid debts — would be restored to the original families. Temporary possessors were to be compensated for any unexhausted improvements they may have made on the land.[5] Concentrated ownership, and the division of society into landed and landless classes, was thereby prevented from creeping into the system. The Jubilee effectively took the profit out of landholding as such, leaving no incentive for speculation.

Parenthetically, North American colonists in Pennsylvania in the 1700s, still recalling well their deprivation of rights in the Old World, expressed the importance of their newly won access to land on what has come to be called the Liberty Bell. They inscribed this now-famous symbol with the opening words of the biblical injunction to institute the Jubilee as a means of preserving freedom: "Proclaim Liberty throughout the land and to all the people thereof" (Lev. 25:10). The founder of Pennsylvania, William Penn, advocated that all men be "tenants to the public," and instituted a tax on land to defray public expenses.[6]

Those who suppose environmental concerns are new to the present age have forgotten the land laws of the Bible. To prevent exhaustion of the land, a periodical fallow was ordered. "During one year in every seven, the soil, left to the influences of sun and frost, wind and rain, was to be allowed to 're-create' itself after six years' cropping, exactly as the tiller of the soil renewed his strength, after six days' work, by his Sabbath day's rest."[7]

As noted, the tribe of Levi did not share in the equal division of the land. The arrangements were fascinating. The Levites were charged with carrying out religious services and other public duties. To bring their ministrations within easy reach of all citizens, they were given official residences and surrounding land in forty-eight cities. This fell far short of the acreage they would have received had they been born into any other tribe. Yet, as humans, they had the same earth rights as the others, so they were entitled to an indemnity from the eleven tribes who received the land that would otherwise have gone to them. This indemnity was given concrete expression in the tithe — one-tenth of the product from the land occupied by the eleven other tribes.

Sharing and Exclusive Private Use — Both at the Same Time

Here, in principle, is the formula for a just land system in almost any time or place. The compensation to the Levites was an arrangement for maintaining the substance of *equal rights* to land, alongside of and compatible with *unequal* physical division of the land itself.

> Fortunately it is not even difficult to assert an equal and common right without physical division. If a father gives his children a cake, they naturally assert their equal rights by cutting it up into equal shares. But if he gives them a pony, they divide, not the pony, but the use of it. If he leaves them a house in equal shares, they may either share the occupancy of the house equally, or occupy the house unequally . . ., paying the rental into a common fund, from which each draws an equal share; or they may let the whole house to someone else and equally divide the rent.[8]

So it is with land. As long as the people share equally in its value (its rent, in economic terminology) through the application of that value to common uses from which all benefit, the private ownership and unequal partition of the land are rendered morally and pragmatically benign.

The modern equivalent of the sin of removing, or "setting back," the neighbor's landmark is not the private *ownership of land*. Rather, it is the private *appropriation of land value*. By disallowing this, society would satisfy in a practical way the most fundamental biblical imperative for economic justice.

It must be evident, however, that the Hebrews' plan of equal physical division among the tribes, apart from the arrangement for the Levites, appears unworkable for modern civilization. While suited to the primitive conditions of the time, it ceases to be feasible when a civilization moves beyond the pastoral or agricultural stage. It is one thing, as portions of land are reshuffled in the Jubilee Year, to roll up one's tents and move on with family and animals. But who would build today's unmovable homes, factories, or shops without secure tenure?

Clearly, the ancient forms need to be replaced with contemporary forms that embrace the principles of the land division and the Jubilee without preventing the sophisticated and relatively permanent improvements on the land that are characteristic of advanced civilizations.

The Profit of the Earth

"The profit of the earth is for all" (Eccles. 5:9). The Old Testament ethic, to assure everyone the same natural opportunity, asserts that all people have an equal right to economic rent.

Some economists and moral theologians seem puzzled to find extremely high land values in poor nations. They fail to pay attention to land monopoly and how owners of vast estates create artificial land shortages that both boost the price of sites and condemn the landless to grinding poverty.

The Levite tithe, as shown, demonstrates how the socialization of economic rent can counterbalance the private and unequal ownership of land, satisfying both ethical and practical requirements. But there is another equally important basis for its advocacy: Rent should be taken by society *because it is a social product*.

This rent or land value arises in large measure from two societal phenomena: the mere presence of population and community activity in a particular area. The more people, the more demand for space on which to live and work, so the higher people bid for the land. Community activity includes such governmental facilities and services as roads, schools, police and fire protection, libraries and parks, sewage and garbage disposal, water and power utilities, plus the totality of private commercial and cultural operations. As these make the setting more attractive and more productive, people again bid more for the land.

Individuals, however, in their bare capacity as landowners, do little or nothing to produce land value. By withholding sites from use, they may generate scarcity, artificially inflating the rent—but this is designated as speculative value, which differs from the real value of land.

Do not an owner's improvements add to the value of his or her land? Yes, but only to the same degree that they may add to that of neighboring land. Conversely, the owner's land may derive less value from its improvements than from the improvements on neighboring land. All this is shown by the fact that adjacent improved and unimproved sites tend to have virtually the same value. In midtown Manhattan, the value of a totally vacant lot is astronomical, simply because of neighboring skyscrapers and the surrounding millions of people. On the other hand, the land under costly Scotty's Castle in Death Valley, California, erected at the behest of an eccentric millionaire, remains about as worthless as the surrounding uninhabited desert. There is no community around it to give it value.

Land Rent Concept Disputed

Defining rent as a distinctively social product has not gone unchallenged. Edwin R. A. Seligman, for example, maintained, inasmuch as nothing can be long produced for sale without public demand, that society creates the value not only of land but of all commodities.[9] George R. Geiger recalls, however, that economic value is determined, not by demand alone, but by the relationship between demand and supply:

> [T]he press of population and all the amenities of civilized society express themselves in the demand for land—as they do in the demand for everything else—but whereas the demand for land *must* raise rent and land value, the value of consumer goods and capital goods will rise *or* fall, not merely as demand varies, but also in proportion to the elasticity of a reproducible supply in meeting that demand.[10]

He illustrates this by pointing out that in large cities, where rent is invariably high, the value of labor products tends to be low, not high. Unlike goods, the supply of land is constant, supremely inelastic. ("Made" land, such as the polders of the Zuider Zee, is more correctly defined as capital; in any case, such "land" is quantitatively infinitesimal, too insignificant to disturb the general proposition.)

> Given an unmonopolized supply of any economic element, in the production of which there is some measure of competition, increased demand and higher societal organization may not result in increased value. But since there is essentially a monopoly of land and since it is fundamentally irreproducible, increasing demand and social organization *must* raise land value.[11]

This hypothesizes an absence of monopoly in consumer and capital goods. However, Seligman asserts that the growth of economic monopolies of all kinds distinguishes the modern age, so the " 'unearned increment' of land is only one instance of a far larger class."[12] He likens increases in land values to the rising earnings of a newspaper, both due to a community's growth. Jackson H. Ralston trenchantly observes that in order for such a parallel to be valid, "the newspaper plant must be closed, the machinery left in place, and all the labor employed in it discharged. In that case, how much unearned increment will the newspaper building and the machinery, now idle, put into the pocket of the owner because they are surrounded by an industrial community?"[13]

Land value is not the only type of unearned increment. The increased value of a company's shares traded after capitalization is usually nothing but a windfall to the purchaser; except in those infrequent cases where he plays an active role in successful policy decisions, his investment does nothing to enhance production. So, also, is the appreciated value of antiques and of rare works of art unearned;[14] like land rent, it represents a monopoly profit. For that matter, inherited talent is unearned, as is inherited energy and health.

Yet shares of stock in genuine capital concerns are subject to market forces; thus, gains are balanced by losses when supply temporarily outstrips demand. Monopolies of rare works of art and craftmanship "do not lay a toll on anybody's labour; they do not affect any of the creative processes upon which the material well-being of millions depends. . . ."[15] Favorable genes are not acquired or enjoyed by depriving others of them. In short, good fortune, while unearned and often undeserved, is not the same as robbery.

Concentrated ownership of capital and consumer goods is, indeed, a feature of our age. But labor and capital can find ways to survive and prosper, circumventing this type of monopoly, *if* access to land is not at the same time locked up. The more pervasive and underlying character of concentrated land ownership is dramatically embodied in Winston Churchill's castigation of land monopoly as "the mother of monopoly."[16] John R. Commons, a contemporary of Seligman, took care to look beneath the surface: "If the size of fortunes is taken into account, it will be found that perhaps ninety-five percent of the total values represented by these millionaire fortunes is due to those investments classed as land values and natural monopolies, and to competitive industries aided by such monopolies."[17] Geiger concludes: "Antaeus-like, capital derives its strength from land, and it would appear that the breaking of land monopoly—which must follow once the value of land has been socialized—might operate upon the very foundations of capitalistic monopoly."[18]

Marx himself made the same point in strong terms: "The monopoly of property in land is even the basis of the monopoly of capital."[19] Numerous passages in part VIII, volume I and part VI, volume III of *Capital* further demonstrate his comprehension that land monopoly underlies, and is the source of, the exploitation of labor.

Why, then, did Marx not support rooting out land monopoly through community collection of land rent, as advocated, for example, by George? It did not fit in with his scheme of history. He realized it would return society to a system of self-earned private property, which he considered primitive and capable only of "universal mediocrity."[20] Marx theorized that inevitably the centralized means of production and the socialization of labor would become incompatible with their capitalist integument or coating, until at last this "integument is burst asunder,"[21] to be replaced by "the associated producers, rationally regulating their interchange with Nature."[22] His vision of collectivism required a dictatorship of the proletariat for an indefinite transition period.[23] Marx wrote:

> The nationalization of land will work a complete change in the rela-
> tions between labor and capital and finally do away altogether with
> capitalist production, whether industrial or rural. Only then the class
> distinctions and privileges will disappear . . . *National centralization of
> the means of production* will become the natural basis of a society
> composed of associations of free and equal producers consciously
> acting upon a common and rational plan.[24]

Marx did not give serious attention to George's proposal for socializing rent without nationalizing land. He dismissed it contemptuously as "simply an attempt, decked out with socialism, to *save capitalist domination* and indeed to *establish it afresh on an even wider basis* than its present one."[25]

Since the socialization of rent would erase land monopoly, and since even Marx admitted that land monopoly was the basis of capital monopoly, his characterization of George's plan becomes intelligible only on the sup-position that Marx's real desire was not to *abolish* monopoly, whether of land or capital, but to transfer it from private owners to the central state. He assumed what decades of Marxist experience have now made difficult to claim, namely, that under the dictatorship of the proletariat, classes — and with them, the state as an instrument of exploitation — would disappear. He also accepted (probably via Hegel) Rousseau's pernicious fallacy that the individual gains freedom through subjection to a whole of which he constitutes a presumedly equal part.[26]

Updating the Mosaic Model

The Mosaic system, as already noted, was attuned to simpler conditions, when the Hebrews were almost exclusively herdsmen and farmers. Univer-sal *principles* of justice embodied by the laws of Moses remain timely; it is the biblical *arrangements* for their implementation that are at cross purposes with the requirements of modern societies. True, the prescription for compensation to the Levites suggests a general method for implementing social justice in any era, but even details of that prescription were adapted to a specific context that does not now obtain.

It was left to Henry George to expound, little more than a century ago, how the essence of the Mosaic model is applicable to the modern age in all its economic aspects—rural or urban, agricultural or industrial, technologically undeveloped or advanced. He did not claim originality for this plan. Although he arrived at it independently, its basic ideas had been put forward earlier by the Physiocrats, the founders of economic science, and Thomas Paine, among others. But George refined the ideas more fully than any of his precursors and argued them more powerfully.

What George advocated was to leave land titles in private hands but to appropriate land values via taxation. "I do not propose either to purchase or to confiscate private property in land. The first would be unjust; the second, needless. . . . *It is not necessary to confiscate land; it is only necessary to confiscate rent.*"[27] A small percentage of the rent would be left to the landowner, enough to facilitate a market in land titles, thus avoiding the burden and expense of auctioning and leasing lands through government agencies.

> The machinery of property assessment and taxation, George points out, is already everywhere at hand. In those states where the value of land is now assessed separately from its improvements, no further preparation is needed; elsewhere, a separate assessment would be undertaken as a first step. Then, in accordance with the enacted legislation, the tax rate on the raw land would be increased by stages until, on completion of the program, approximately the full annual ground rent would thus be recaptured as public revenue. . . . Coordinately with each stage, other existing taxes—those on improvements, personal property, commodities and services, private and corporate income, and so on—would be commensurately reduced until [ideally] they were eliminated entirely.[28]

The mechanics are simple, in theory and in practice, as will be shown. Land assessments, in accord with the best accepted professional standards, are determined by the market—what people are willingly paying for land. No owner or tenant is expropriated or evicted. No limit is placed on the quantity of land one may hold, as long as the annual tax is paid. As under most property tax systems, tenure is at risk only if tax delinquencies occur. Landowners are not compensated for the loss of their prior practice of taking the lion's share of socially created values; but neither are they obliged to reimburse the public for previous gains at society's expense.

Once laws are enacted to carry out this approach, no technical or administrative barriers block the full collection of land rent in states where the tax on land is now low or nonexistent. To avoid economic disruption and minimize opposition, a system of land-value taxation may be instituted gradually. Interestingly, to implement the process over forty years would be tantamount to incremental compensation without interest.[29] However, it would be unduly solicitous of landed interests for society to move that slowly in fully capturing what belongs to it by right. On the other hand, responsible advocates do not urge precipitate imposition of the change.

Economists who call for public capture of land values tend to focus on land as "space on the earth's surface." Yet they recognize that land also includes subsurface mineral deposits, radio frequencies, television channels, air rights, waterways, seabeds, wind and solar power, and so forth. Wherever and whenever these exhibit economic value, their value belongs to all people equally and should be captured, so far as practicable, for society. Appropriation methods other than an annual tax may be expedient—whether severance taxes, special benefit charges, auction of leases, or other approaches that seem appropriate.

Part of a Grand Design

As a liberationist, George considered his remedy no mere human contrivance. He saw the growth of land value and the easy means of equitably distributing it as an expression of benevolent supernatural design:

> In a rude state of society where there is no need for common expenditure, there is no value attaching to land. . . . But as civilization goes on, as a division of labor takes place, as men come into centres, so do the common wants increase and so does the necessity for public revenue arise. And so in that value which attaches to land, not by reason of anything the individual does, but by reason of the growth of the community, is a provision intended—we may safely say *intended*—to meet that social want. Just as society grows, so do the common needs grow, and so grows this value attaching to land—the provided fund from which they can be supplied.[30]

Only reluctantly did George accept the term "Single Tax" that others gave to his proposal. What he envisaged is not really a tax at all, in the sense of a levy upon production, but rather, as Rybeck aptly puts it, a "super user charge"—a fee paid for the special privilege of exclusive access to a natural good.[31] Nor did George regard "singleness" an essential feature; his system does not exclude the possibility of public charges for other special benefits. He only held that those who enjoy special benefits at the expense of all should pay for these before other charges are imposed.[32]

Whether called a Single Tax or a land value tax, this description does not begin to capture the liberating scope of the concept. Collecting land rent lifts a heavy burden off all wealth producers, especially the poor. It removes the need for onerous taxes on labor's wages, consumers' purchases, and businesses' profits. Even more importantly, it shields society from injustice: It deprives landlords of the ability to exact a parasitic ransom from everyone else. Its object is the realization of the biblical ideal: "They shall build houses and inhabit them; and they shall plant vineyards, and eat the fruit of them. They shall not build, and another inhabit; they shall not plant, and another eat" (Isa. 65:21–23; *see also* Prov. 27:18 and 1 Cor. 9:7–10).

Earmarks of a "Good Tax"

Considered as a tax, George's remedy satisfies eminently the classic criteria for a good tax that have been accepted since the days of Adam Smith.

It does not discourage the production of wealth. It stimulates production. It unburdens producers, as noted above. And by imposing a charge on unused and poorly used sites, it gives the owners a compelling incentive either to put their land to appropriate use or make it available to others who will.

> Tax manufactures, and the effect is to check manufacturing; tax improvements, and the effect is to lessen improvement; tax commerce, and the effect is to prevent exchange; tax capital, and the effect is to drive it away. But the whole value of land may be taken in taxation, and the only effect will be to stimulate industry, to open new opportunities to capital, and to increase the production of wealth.[33]

It is easy and cheap to collect. To collect most of the land value requires no more administrative machinery than to collect a small fraction of it, as is usually now done. To abolish taxes concurrently on real estate improvements simplifies the assessment process. As the recapture of socially created land values paves the way to the *un*taxing of production, the elimination of monstrous bureaucracies now in place for collecting taxes on incomes, wages, imports, sales, and so forth will lead to great public savings.

It provides a reliable source of funding. Its certainty "partakes of the immovable and inconcealable nature of the land itself."[34] With assessment rolls readily available for inspection, and with public scrutiny focused on them because of the primacy of land values as other sources of taxation are increasingly eschewed, this levy lends itself to easy surveillance and enforcement by both officials and taxpayers themselves. Busey, a specialist in Latin American politics and economics, correctly observes that no social program can succeed "apart from supportive attitudes and institutions."[35] Yet, for the reasons cited, this type of tax program is more evasion-proof than most.

With the speculative water squeezed out of land values, and public revenue wholly or largely derived from rent, would this not mean a sharp reduction in the funding available for public purposes? Not so. The evidence demonstrates that while a sufficiently heavy land-value tax will cause speculative value to decrease even to the point of disappearance, productive use will be so stimulated (especially if the tax is combined with a corresponding reduction in the levy on improvements) that aggregate use value soon exceeds the aggregate speculative value that formerly obtained.[36]

It cannot be shifted. A tax on land values cannot be shifted from the landowner to the landuser through a rent increase. Since something close to the full annual market value of a site must be paid to the community, regardless of whether or not the site is being put to optimal use, the owner is provided with a compelling incentive either to put it to such use himself or make it available to someone who will. Under such circumstances, for him to hold land for speculation would be senseless. He cannot shift the payment to the user by a raise in rent, since he obviously cannot charge more than market value. If he chooses to retain title to the site while it is used by someone else, he simply passes the rent on to the community, less a small percentage as his fee for serving as collector. (Incidentally, Georgists have sometimes been accused of wanting to force *all* land into use; no Georgist advocates such an absurdity but only that land be put to its highest and best use, which, in the case of most marginal and all submarginal land, would be to no use at all.)

It is equitable. "[I]t falls only upon those who receive from society a peculiar and valuable benefit, and upon them in proportion to the benefit they receive. It is the taking by the community for the use of the community, of that value which is the creation of the community. It is the application of the common property to common uses."[37]

Rent, as a social product, should be returned to the community. Does justice then demand that interest from capital which is occasionally derived indirectly from rent also be appropriated by the community? Perhaps so in theory. But there is no practical way to separate such capital from the bulk of capital, which is simply stored-up labor.

This need not disconcert those who are more eager to stop current wrongs and prevent future wrongs than to punish old wrongs. Once severed from its landed base and unsupported by political favoritism that insulates it from competition, the advantage afforded by possession of capital cannot be long sustained except through the *use* of it in ways that redound to the felicity of the public. Under these circumstances, accumulations of capital are soon dissipated unless they are directed toward the satisfaction of people's wants. The old adage, "from shirtsleeves to shirtsleeves in three generations," derives precisely from seeing capitalist fortunes dissolved in this fashion.

The "felicity of the public" alludes not to some visionary standard but to the choices people freely make — or, in economic jargon, to their perceived marginal utility. How advertising distorts choices and degrades popular taste has been properly censured by Vance Packard.[38] Yet, do we prefer to trust in the wisdom and refinement of some elite that will dictate what goods and services we should be allowed? Or is human welfare better served by market democracy, where one need not be in a majority for his vote to count, and where the fulfillment of popular desires that we may disdain as tawdry does not preclude the availability of quality to those who seek and are willing to pay for it?[39]

A few words need to be said here about the impact of George's remedy upon the rate of interest. The rate of pure interest is determined by many and often complex variables, but the public appropriation of rent tends to drive it down. Wealth will not be invested as capital unless it yields thereby a return at least as high as it would obtain if invested in land, plus a premium ("insurance") for risk and depreciation. If more wealth is made available as capital because nothing can be gained by investing it in land (rent being publicly appropriated), the rate of interest, all other things remaining equal, will decrease. The net effect of this will be to increase wages – both by stimulating the demand for labor by diverting wealth from sterile to productive use, and by making it easier for workers to acquire the means to go into business for themselves. The foregoing treatment of the rate of interest (which departs from that of George, but strengthens the case for his policy proposal) is supported by the analysis of the 1988 Nobel laureate in economics, Maurice Allais.[40]

Will the unburdening of labor and production lead to equality of wealth? No. A full-scale application of the remedy may be anticipated to reduce greatly the huge gaps that now separate rich and poor, but it will not assure equal incomes to all citizens. This side of the Kingdom of Heaven, differences in productive capacity and performance will necessarily be reflected by differences in income.

Even Marx admitted the inevitability of this in the "first phase" of communist society – i.e., this side of the "higher phase," which was his secular version of the Kingdom.[41] The market is an imperfect adjudicator of differences in people's capacity and performance. Critics from Marx to Marcuse have subjected it to adverse and often penetrating analysis, yet what they offer in its place is infinitely worse. The market, if purged of monopoly, affords more scope for human liberation than anything socialism, in any of its forms, has yet devised.

A Constructive Answer to Dependency Theory

Toward the end of chapter 6, we made the statement that "even insofar as dependency theory is (in a limited sense) analytically correct, the social ills to which it calls attention could be substantially dispelled by the proper allocation of rent or land values." This approach, moreover, affords a way of addressing them that is far more practical and constructive than is the erection of trade barriers or legal restriction of foreign ownership. An Australian writer explains why:

> When investors purchase real estate they are seeking RENT, and the rent they seek is not paid for the use of buildings, machinery, et cetera. Rather it is GROUND rent—that is, rent paid for the use of LAND.
>
> Building rent is of marginal use to an investor. Office blocks, hotels and shopping centres must be maintained, and replaced periodically, if they are to go on yielding rent. Therefore, landlords do not become rich through buying and letting buildings, because much of their building rent is absorbed as labor costs. At the same time, a nation does not suffer if building rent leaves the country, because most of it returns eventually—as the buildings are repaired and/or replaced.
>
> Site rent is totally different. Site rent is not earned by the investor. Instead, site rent—like the land values on which it depends—is created by everyone in each village, town, city or nation. Therefore site rent appears, and flows into landowners' pockets—without effort on their part—while ever the nation remains inhabited. Furthermore, if a nation prospers, or becomes more populous, then its ground yields an ever-increasing quantity of rent.
>
> Hence, when investors from one country buy property in other countries they are seeking SITE RENT, which they hope to obtain directly from tenants, or indirectly by selling land in the future when its price or capital value has increased. . . .
>
> The site rent that is so attractive to overseas investors can be kept in the country quite easily—*by shifting taxation from labor onto land.*[42]

Foreshadowning of the Promised Land: Putting Antiexploitation Policies to Work

Cited earlier was the spectacular economic transformation over the past two decades of five nations on the Asian Pacific Rim: Japan, Hong Kong, Singapore, South Korea, and Taiwan. Since land policies promoting enterprise were among the factors that fostered their rapid rise from abysmal poverty to vibrant prosperity, it is germane now to examine some strengths and weaknesses of these policies.

Looking first at *Japan*, it has been claimed but not yet fully documented that its economic "miracle" owes much to the carry-over impact of a somewhat flawed land-value tax implemented briefly a century ago during the Meiji Restoration.[43] More certain is that the Japanese success could not have taken place without the land reform imposed during the postwar allied occupation under General Douglas MacArthur. This is not to downgrade the importance of related policies, such as the enactment of low tax rates on savings and investments. Japan's land reform was exclusively agrarian. Its purpose was the conversion of tenants into small proprietors, breaking the stranglehold of the hereditary landed oligarchs and giving the average peasant a personal stake in the economy. In this it was most effective. It opened up to a broad segment of the population the drive to produce and save, and this fueled the nation's resurgence.

Today, the momentum of that resurgence continues for a variety of other reasons. However, the beneficial influence of the land reform was only temporary. Its ultimate effect was not to abolish the privileged class but to create a larger one. This new power class often uses its political muscle to the general detriment, for example, by severely restricting imports and keeping food prices high.

Worse, since the reform did nothing to inhibit speculation, Japan's very progress, with its accompanying industrialization and urbanization, has pushed land prices to astronomical levels. According to the Long-Term Credit Bank of Japan, by 1988 the market value of land in Japan (an area smaller than California) was five times that of land values in the entire United States.[44] In 1990, the land under the gardens and buildings of Tokyo's Imperial Palace alone was "valued at about $70 billion—more than all the land in Florida."[45]

The bulk of profits from this land boom, unfortunately, have not been flowing into the public treasury but into the hands of the parasitical minority fortunate enough to own real estate. All of this underscores the long-range futility of a land reform that addresses itself only to rural acreage, not urban areas, and provides merely for the division and redistribution of holdings, not for a continuous equitable sharing of the peoples' earth rights.

Hong Kong and *Singapore* are special cases due to the fact that the freehold of so much of the land is vested in the Crown (or, as regards Singapore, the Crown's successor). With respect to Hong Kong, Ian Barron presents a convincing argument that the colony's prosperity rests to a considerable measure on the availability of unallocated Crown land, which has acted to constrain the speculative withholding of land held on long-term lease: Large areas of "new" land were brought into use.

Land in new towns was set aside for appropriate community needs . . . whilst that allocated for private development for housing, industry and commercial purposes was sold by public auction and leases. . . . The revenue from the sale of these leases more than repaid the cost of all the works. Thus the site set aside for public use was obtained at no cost to the general taxpayer and indeed the new town development normally produced a profit at an early stage. Undoubtedly the availability of land on this basis—the process of building new towns started in the fifties continues today—has contributed greatly to the economic success which Hong Kong represents.[46]

Under Sir Stamford Raffles in the early nineteenth century, and for some time thereafter, ground rent was virtually the sole source of public revenue in Singapore. This has long since ceased to be true, but a combination of unusual circumstances and technical provisions produced an effect comparable to that of straightforward land value taxation. These include: the reversion of full title to the republic of much land held under 99-year leaseholds, now expired; the high magnitude of the property tax as a percentage of annual value, together with incentives in the form of sizeable twenty-year tax abatements for approved development and rehabilitation; eminent domain provisions that make it easy and cheap for the republic to acquire land for public purposes and risky for owners to undervalue their holdings for tax purposes.

South Korea captures substantial ground rent through a differential levy on "capital" gains. This represents a mode of land-value taxation which, however oblique and partial, has had significant results in spurring production and equalizing the blessings of economic progress. Underassessment, however, has operated partially to negate these gains, and the economy, once flourishing, is threatened by stagflation.

Of these five countries, *Taiwan* has the most complete and unambiguous system of land value taxation. This is not surprising. Dr. Sun Yat-sen, revered as the founder of modern China, was an avowed proponent. In an interview with American journalists, he is quoted as saying: "The teaching of your single-taxer, Henry George, will be the basis of our program of reform."[47] Sun got the principle included in the platform of his party, the Kuomintang, but was unable to implement it in his lifetime. Events then took a tragic course as Japanese invasion, war, civil war, and Communist takeover followed in succession.

But the Chinese who fled the mainland to Taiwan carried in their hearts and minds Sun's land policies and incorporated them in their new constitution. Taiwan's approach covers both rural and urban land and has been characterized as "the most successful of postwar land reforms."[48] In addition to large-scale redistribution, the system is marked by a tax on the unimproved value of land (based on self-assessment), with a separate tax at higher rates on vacant and underimproved sites. Also, a steeply graduated land-value increment tax is imposed on increases in value over a ten-year period, and at time of sale.

As early as 1967, ten years before the plan went into full operation in its present form, C. F. Koo, president of the Chinese National Association of Industry and Commerce, concluded that the first stages had already performed a critical role in encouraging the island's transformation. He explained that, before the land reform, landlords were unwilling to invest in industry, for they had no incentive to do so. They could prosper by underpaying tenants and by reaping unearned land values. The land reform, Koo said, greatly minimized both of these forms of exploitation, "thus removing the obstacle that stood in the way of industrial development and creating a remarkable change in the structure of the social economy."[49]

Far to the south of Japan and the "four little tigers," as they have been called, are two English-speaking nations, also on the Pacific Rim, that have experienced land value taxation over a much longer span of time.

The public appropriation of land values in *Australia* began on a small scale in 1878. In the same year, the government of Sir George Grey in *New Zealand* enacted a levy on the unimproved value of land, but it was revoked by a new ministry before ever being put into effect. By the turn of the century, however, land value taxation had taken firm root in both nations. Certain local traditions and the dire need to protect farmland from urban invasion created a favorable climate, but George's writings and a three-month lecture tour there in 1890 exerted a powerful influence. Today the two commonwealths present the most definitive demonstration of land value taxation in practice.

The social utility of Australia's substantial but modified land value tax was revealed in a survey comparing the three states that have much heavier land value taxes and much lower improvement taxes with the other three. During the half century covered by the survey, the first group — Queensland, New South Wales, and Western Australia — saw more land put under crops, while the second group — South Australia, Victoria, and Tasmania — experienced decreases. The value of improvements as compared to land, indicating the degree of construction, was 151 percent in the first group as against only 79 percent in the second; it was highest of all, 198 percent, in Queensland, which collected the greatest proportion of economic rent. The first group enjoyed higher factory wages, more purchasing power, a greater volume of retail sales, higher capital investment in plant and machinery, more housing construction, and greater increases in assets of financial institutions and cooperative societies. Another critical finding — the flow of population from the second group to the first — revealed that people found superior opportunities where taxes were derived to a greater extent from the growth in land values than from production. Again, Queensland saw the heaviest inflow of people.[50] More recent research confirms the continued thrust and pertinence of the survey's remarkable findings.[51]

Land reformers around the world could profit from paying more attention to Australia and New Zealand. They make widespread use of a property tax collected entirely from land or site values, whereas homes, commercial structures, and other improvements on the land are wholly exempt from taxation. In Queensland, an estimated 51 percent of annual site value was being recaptured as of 1977. The hefty site value tax in Sydney, Australia's largest city, is credited with generating concentrated private renewal of the central city, discouraging land speculation, and providing a healthy public revenue base;[52] whereas Melbourne, which lacks the site value tax, has spotty growth patterns and a business district that fails to compete with commercial growth in the outskirts.[53]

Through local option, in elections where, surprisingly, only landowners are entitled to vote, the site value tax system has been adopted by 65 percent of the municipal councils; these governments control 93 percent of Australia's taxable area. In New Zealand, 80 percent of local jurisdictions use the site value (or, as they call it, "unimproved value") as the sole basis of their property tax.[54]

Other limited but noteworthy applications of the concept may be found around the world. Denmark taxes land values on a national basis, Jamaica on a local basis. Some South African and Western Canadian localities use elements of a site value tax. In the United States, at least fifteen Pennsylvania cities (including Pittsburgh, the second-largest municipality, and Harrisburg, the capital) now tax land values at substantially higher rates than they do buildings. Several California irrigation districts used site value levies to pay for dams and water distribution systems, only to discover that this revenue device helped to break up huge Spanish-style ranches and to favor growth of highly productive smaller farms.

These are only some of the most salient examples, detailed accounts of which would fill another volume. Still another volume might show how the free land and homestead policies that set a young United States on a path of dynamic and relatively equitable economic growth approximated conditions that Moses, Paine, and George wanted society to enjoy throughout all generations — all in contrast to monopolistic land policies, such as those of Latin America, that have obstructed the road to justice there for five centuries.

Suffice it to say here that, while the land value tax theory has nowhere been *fully* implemented, it has been tried sufficiently to provide ample empirical data on which to base judgments. It has worked wherever it has been tried, to the extent it has been tried. The few instances of its abandonment have been occasioned not by failure on its part, but by the influence of highly financed special interests operating in a climate of public ignorance and apathy — as when Hawaii's powerful landowners killed a modest site value tax initiated at the time statehood was gained.

Nobody should expect enlightened land policies alone to usher in the Promised Land. Many other factors may undercut the benefits of such policies. As proof one need only observe the negative impacts of under-assessment in South Korea, Singapore, and Taiwan; of protectionism in Japan; of apartheid in South Africa; of crushing national taxes in Jamaica; of socialistic elements in Australia and New Zealand, and of distorting subsidies in United States cities. We emphatically do not suggest that conditions in any of the places cited — or anywhere else, for that matter — are ideal. What can confidently be asserted is that, were it not for the enlightened land measures earlier described, conditions in those areas would be far worse. These policies have contributed to the material uplift of multitudes of people. Perhaps we do not exaggerate in holding that they foreshadow, in however fragmentary or diluted a form, the cardinal economic lineaments of the Promised Land.

Commons without Tragedy

In the Third World, but also in developed nations, the liberal ideal — the reign of equal rights for all with special privilege for none — awaits fulfillment. The Georgist formulation of the biblical model would, if put into thoroughgoing operation, mean the extirpation of monopoly in a framework of political and economic liberty. It would render free enterprise truly free. All who were willing and able to work could achieve a reasonable degree of economic well-being and security. It would eliminate overprivilege and underprivilege, leaving only such social divisions as might reflect disparate talents, ambitions, values, and other personal characteristics. These conclusions are borne out by effects of the modest applications of the model used to date.

In few places has the power of the landed aristocracy been fully broken. More often its ranks have been augmented or supplanted by new landowners who assumed the interests of the old class. The advance of liberalism, however, signaled a rise in the general standard of living that could not be satisfactorily explained in terms of Marxist theory.[55] The laboring masses became actual or potential members of the petit bourgeoisie. By income or outlook, they entered the middle class. Feeling they had a stake in the existing order, they developed little taste for revolution. This was clearly seen in regions where a real frontier retarded land monopoly and offered opportunities to people, regardless of their inherited status. This, above all, accounts for the fact that Marxism has made so little headway among blue-collar workers in the United States, Canada, Australia, and the like.

Unless the liberal ideal is carried to its logical next step, correcting humanity's economic relationship with the earth, severe land monopoly will surely reassert itself, along with the class divisions and frictions that already are becoming familiar even in many of the presumably advanced democratic and capitalist societies.

A tactical blunder that hobbled the advance of this next step was made by George himself when he asserted, *"We must make land common property."*[56] Although he took pains later to clarify his meaning, the statement has been used by his antagonists with deadly effect to portray him as an advocate of nationalizing land.

Nationalization, with its collectivization and regimentation, was not at all what George favored. By "common property in land," he meant that all people should be assured their equal rights to land, not that they should use it collectively (except in such obviously public functions as roads or parks). He certainly did not intend to signify that land is a common resource to be exploited individually without concern for social consequences, including consequences to later generations, as was alleged by Garrett Hardin to have been the case with the common lands that existed in England until the middle of the nineteenth century.[57]

Hardin, in his provocative and widely mentioned article, "The Tragedy of the Commons,"[58] speaks of the inherent tendency of individuals, each in the rational pursuit of his own interests, to overgraze, denude, and use the commons as a cesspool. That which belongs to everybody in this sense is, indeed, in danger of being valued and maintained by nobody. The enclosure movement ultimately brought an end to this ecologically destructive process, but not without exacting a baneful price in human misery, literally pushing people off the land, that might well be termed "The Tragedy of the Enclosures."

George hit upon a way of securing the benefits of both commons and enclosures, while at the same time avoiding their evils. It is a way which Hardin himself, perhaps unwittingly, endorses in his article:

> During the Christmas shopping season [in Leominster, Massachusetts] the parking meters downtown were covered with plastic bags that bore tags reading: "Do not open until after Christmas. Free parking courtesy of the mayor and city council." In other words, facing the prospect of an increased demand for already scarce space, the city fathers reinstituted the system of the commons.

By calling this a "retrogressive act," Hardin evinces his belief that the meters ought to have been left in operation. Now, parking meter fees exemplify, in specialized form, the public appropriation of land values: They constitute payment for the privilege of temporarily monopolizing a site — compensation to the members of the community whose opportunity to use the site is extinguished for a given time.

Much more than compensation is involved here. If meter fees, instead of being used to pay for community services, were buried in the ground, their collection would still be justified as a means of keeping monopoly temporary and innocuous. Paying for the parking space retains the communal quality of the commons while maximizing the private incentive features of the enclosures.

So too with land value taxation in its more generalized application. By removing any incentive to hoard and speculate in land, and by putting all members of society on an equal footing, its collection would be warranted in terms of social justice and well-being, even if its yield were cast into the sea.

A Socialization Essential to Private Enterprise

Land value taxation rectifies distribution so that all receive wealth in proportion to their contribution to its production. This liberates the economic system from exploiters who contribute little or nothing. Apportioning the wealth pie fairly almost magically results in increasing the size of the pie. And, instead of being a cruel contest in which the cards are stacked against most players because of gross disparities in bargaining power, the market becomes in practice what capitalist theory alleges it to be — a profoundly cooperative process of voluntary exchange of goods and services.

By now it should be evident that when we raised objections to socialism, we were not claiming that *nothing* should be socialized. Paradoxical though it may seem, the only way in which the individual may be assured what properly belongs to him is for society to take what properly belongs to it: The Jeffersonian ideal of individualism requires for its actualization the socialization of rent.

Neither can private enterprise be free if the private appropriation of rent prevails. In those circumstances, landowners always demand their "cut" for giving others access to a portion of nature landowners did not create. When landlords take something for nothing, the portion of wealth that goes to them becomes a stifling tax on enterprise. It comes off the backs of producers, both labor and capital.

Just as orthodox Marxists err, then, in insisting that *everything* be socialized, extreme capitalists often err in insisting that *everything* (even public parks and forests!) be privatized. The middle way is to recognize society's claim to what nature and society create — the value of land and its rent — so that working people, which term certainly does not exclude entrepreneurs, may claim their full share of what they create.

What the world awaits, therefore, is not a confusing welter of compromises and half-measures but a genuinely radical approach in the original and most basic meaning of that term. This is simply the installation of a system of untaxing production combined with the public collection of community-created land values.

In this approach can be found the authentic verities respectively inherent in individualism and socialism. They are organically combined without detriment to the integrity of either. What the individual holds in private and what the community holds (or reaps the benefit of) in common have a clear and logical relationship: Each pole is balanced and complemented by the other.

10

Epilogue

The Promised Land and the Kingdom of God

After the children of Israel had claimed the Promised Land, making good their claim by instituting under Joshua the structural features of a just commonwealth, they turned from the ways of righteousness, lusting after vain attractions and base fancies, and placing their trust in false deities.

> And I brought you into a plentiful land
> to enjoy its fruits and its good things.
> But when you came in you defiled my land,
> and made my heritage an abomination (Jer. 2:7).

The Promised Land, like Eden, is a place of unhindered scope in which to glorify God and manifest his will. But it is not the Kingdom of God. It represents liberation from external bondage—from oppression and restricted access to material opportunity. It is the temporal matrix within which the Kingdom may find full expression. But it is not itself the Kingdom.

It is no reproach to Henry George that he lost sight of this distinction, enraptured by his vision of a just society:

> With want destroyed; with greed changed to noble passions; with the fraternity that is born of equality taking the place of the jealousy and fear that now array men against each other; with mental power loosed by conditions that give to the humblest comfort and leisure; and who shall measure the heights to which our civilization may soar? Words fail the thought! It is the Golden Age of which poets have sung and high-raised seers have told in metaphor! It is the glorious vision which has always haunted men with gleams of fitful splendor. It is what he saw whose eyes at Patmos were closed in a trance. It is the culmination

of Christianity—the City of God on earth, with its walls of jasper and its gates of pearl! It is the reign of the Prince of Peace![1]

Another Dimension: Inner Life

The sublimity of that rhapsodic paean should not blind us to the sober truth that God's reign is not achievable through any outward system. Although it is a heresy that locates this Kingdom exclusively in the afterlife or identifies it with some ethereal paradise, Jesus declared it to be "not of this world" (John 18:36) but "within" (Luke 17:21).

The preeminence of this "Kingdom within"[2] makes it in essence triumphant over all the powers that assail it. This is one of the deeper meanings of the Resurrection. But the Resurrection cannot be interpreted to justify the treachery of Judas, the cruelty of Caiaphas, the cynicism of Pilate, or the fickleness of the Jerusalem mob. No more than St. Paul's "Prison Epistles" or Bunyan's *Pilgrim's Progress* or the *Ethics* of Dietrich Bonhoeffer or *The Diary of Anne Frank* can be read as arguments in favor of the circumstances under which they were brought into being.

> Behind the barbed wire of the concentration camp the old man presses his priceless store of powdered milk upon the wan mother and her sickly child. Behind the bars of Reading Gaol the prisoner feels the murderer's fate as if it were his own. In the House of the Dead compassion lives. It lives in the tapping of a monocle against a cell wall; in the crumpled note, furtively secreted; in the muffled whisper, exhorting, "Courage!" Where love is present it will find a way to manifest itself. But surely it is not God's will that human brotherhood be limited to cramped, clandestine modes of demonstration. A tap on the wall, a whisper in the night—these may be earnests of the fullness of the Kingdom, but they are also prophetic judgments upon any social order which necessitates them.[3]

By equalizing opportunity, political and economic liberation tend to draw both poor and rich into the middle class. As an expression of social justice, this constitutes genuine advance, ethical as well as material. But it is not an unalloyed spiritual gain.

The middle-class ethos is marked by characteristic virtues: industry, thrift, restraint, commercial and professional rectitude. It is also marked by low prudentialism, self-satisfaction, and an inclination to regard material well-being as a sign of righteousness.

Hence, even (or perhaps especially) in the Promised Land, the process of what Freire calls "conscientization"[4] (roughly, consciousness-raising through social commitment), emphasized and refined by liberation theology, must continue, although in a different vein. For the Kingdom of God will flourish only when the outward liberation exhibited by the ascent of the poor to the material level of bourgeois existence becomes an inward liberation, a victory over the limitations of the bourgeois ethos.

With that very major caveat, let us conclude by recapitulating the essence of a strategy for achieving economic, if not spiritual, liberation. Let those seeking genuine social uplift realize that it is radical bedrock ethics — not mere poetic fluff — to reaffirm with all the strength that can be mustered the inspiring words from Psalm 24: *The earth is the Lord's, and the fulness thereof.*

"The Earth Is the Lord's"

This is not an isolated statement in the Bible but is again embodied in the institution of the Jubilee, in the prohibition against removing ancient landmarks, and in the decree that the land should not be sold forever. The prophets had it in mind when they inveighed against those who laid field to field. And it appears in Ecclesiastes 5:9, whose author wrote that "the profit of the earth is for all."

To say that "the earth is the Lord's" tells us something about God. It tells us that he is like a dirt farmer. He is attached to the land and loves it. By no means is he a spiritual abstraction removed from the world and oblivious to this Wasteland in which we live. There is, so to speak, dirt under God's fingernails. He is concerned with everyday happenings and with things that can be touched, with what goes on in the field, the factory, the courthouse, the exchange. God is the maker of a world of eating and sleeping, working and begetting. He loves this world so much that he himself became flesh and blood for its salvation. In this sense, God is eminently materialistic.

Further, it tells us that God does not consider politics and economics subjects too crass for his notice. We blaspheme if we imagine him a capricious tyrant who has imposed an order that condemns children to die of hunger and retirees to subsist on cat food while others diet to lose weight while feeding steak to their pets. It is *people* who have enjoined this order in denial of his sovereignty and in defiance of his demand for righteousness.

To say that "the earth is the Lord's" not only indicates something about God, it indicates something about his land. It was evident to biblical writers that God had provided the land as a storehouse of natural opportunity for humankind. It was not to be monopolized or despoiled or treated as speculative merchandise but was rather to be used reverently, and conserved dutifully, and, above all, maintained as a source from which every person by the application of his labor might sustain himself in decent comfort. It was seen as an inalienable trust, which no individual or class could legitimately appropriate so as to exclude others, and which no generation could legitimately barter away. Thus, Naboth the Jezreelite refused to sell or trade his vineyard to Ahab because "the Lord forbade it" (1 Kings 21:3), and Jeremiah redeemed his cousin's field at Anathoth because God demanded it (Jer. 32:6–10).

To say that "the earth is the Lord's" also tells us something about man's place in the world. With the recognition that the true owner of the land is God, it follows that every person has a right to the produce which equitable usufruct has yielded to his efforts. As the apostle Paul put it, if the ox has a right to a share in the grain which it treads out, surely a human being must have a right to the fruits of his labor (1 Cor. 9:8–11).

The allegory of the Tenants in the Vineyard (Matt. 21:33–46; Mark 12:1–12; Luke 20:9–18) reveals that this works both ways: Jesus clearly assumes that the tenants' right to the fruit of their labor should be coupled with the recognition of God's claim to the vineyard.[5] Perhaps the question that liberationists and all seekers after justice should ask is, "How can a person fulfill his duty to God if he be denied, on the one hand, fair access to nature, the raw material without which there can be no wealth, and, on the other, the full and free ownership of his own labor and its earnings?"

To recognize that "the earth is the Lord's" is to see that the same God who established communities has also in his providence ordained for them, through the land itself, a just source of revenue. And yet, in the topsy-turvy Wasteland in which we live, the income from this source goes mainly into the pockets of speculators and monopolists, while communities or governments meet their needs by extorting from individual producers the fruits of honest toil. If ever there were any doubt that structural sin exists, our present system of taxation is the proof. Everywhere about us, we see the ironic spectacle of government penalizing the individual for his industry and initiative and taking away from him a share of that which he produces, yet at the same time lavishing upon the nonproducer undeserved windfalls which, in truth, the community produces. The socially produced value of the land is reaped by the speculators in exact proportion to the land which they withhold. The greater the Wasteland, the greater the reward.

Liberation theologians are absolutely right to question a system that allows a man — perhaps a civic leader and a pillar of his church — to sit back with perfect respectability and collect thousands, even millions, of dollars in unearned increments created by the public for withholding land from those who wish (and desperately need) to put it to productive use.

Think about this also: If that same person improves his site — to beautify the neighborhood, provide goods for consumers and jobs for workers, or create housing for fellow townspeople — instead of being treated as a public benefactor, he will be fined as if he were a criminal, in the form of heavier taxes. What kind of justice is this? Does it comport with any divine plan or the notion of human rights, or does it not, rather, perpetuate the Wasteland?

Toward a Victimless Society

Acquisitiveness, or to use another term, the "profit motive," is a well-nigh universal fact of human nature. In focusing attention upon land monopolists and speculators, we do not mean to suggest that they have any corner on it. Even when we speak of them as "parasites," it is to show how an unfair and evil *system* is operating; it is not to single *them* out for personal moral condemnation. They are not necessarily more greedy or personally sinful than are people at large, except to the extent that they knowingly obstruct reforms aimed at removing the basis of exploitation. Many are simply abiding by the dictum: "If one has to live under a corrupt system, it is better to be a beneficiary than a victim of it."

But no one should have to live under a corrupt system. The profit motive can be channeled in ways that are socially desirable as well as in ways that are socially destructive.

Let us give testimony to our faith that the earth is the Lord's by doing everything we can to build a social order in which there are no victims.

Appendix

A Liberationist for All Seasons — Henry George:
A Study in the Marriage of Theoria *and* Praxis

Henry George devised so creative and comprehensive a way to free humanity from its ancient and chronic social inequities that he may be likened to a modern Moses. But who was this man?[1]

Early in this book, George is identified as a "political economist and social philosopher," which he surely was. Yet he could properly be called a theologian. Not only are all his books suffused with a deep spiritual feeling. More than that, they have theodicy — "the justification of the ways of God to man" — as at least part of their objective. His most famous work, *Progress and Poverty*, closes with an argument for personal immortality, and even his most technical economic treatise, *The Science of Political Economy*, contains many passages (including virtually the whole of book I, chapter 7) that seek to demonstrate the presence of divine will behind the natural order. In many respects, he was a liberation theologian a century before the term came into vogue.

George is also identified as a reformer, but this term is too pallid to convey fully either the radical nature of his doctrine or the intensity of his commitment to it. Although certainly no advocate of violence, he might truly be called a social revolutionist. The Duke of Argyll, in an intended put-down, styled him a "prophet," an appellation he accepted as a badge of honor. He was, at any rate, a Christian activist, in whose life and writings *theoria* and *praxis* were never separated.

Formative Years — Schooled in Hardship

George was born in 1839 in Philadelphia, the second of ten children of devout evangelical parents of British ancestry. His father was a small-scale publisher of prayer books and Sunday school literature for the Episcopal Church; his mother, a former schoolmistress. His formal education ended when he was not yet fourteen.

Sensitive to a decline in his father's business, the boy secured menial employment in a china shop and later in the office of a marine adjuster.

But he was definitely not culturally deprived. He had been brought up in a "genteel household" where Shakespeare, poetry, history, and travel were part of the regular literary diet, together with constant exposure to the Bible. An ardent reader, he made copious use of the Quaker Apprentice's Library, attended popular scientific lectures at the Franklin Institute, and formed a club at which he and his friends avidly discussed topics ranging from Aristophanes and Byron to Mormonism.

At fifteen, the restless youth sailed as foremast hand to Australia and India. His letters and journal of the voyage give evidence of his ripening powers of observation, his sympathy for victims of poverty and arbitrary power, and the beginnings of what was to become a literary style unsurpassed by any nonfiction writer of his century. He returned mature beyond his years.

Back in Philadelphia, George found times were growing hard and prospects for advancement on the eastern seaboard, slim. Thinking to better himself in a less settled region, he worked his way as a steward aboard a steamer through the Strait of Magellan to San Francisco. But by then depression had hit the West Coast, too. He tried his hand as a storekeeper and prospector, printer, weigher in a rice mill, and itinerant farmhand, then mostly as a journeyman typographer. He became a union member, and also joined the Methodist Church.

Having just come of age, George met and courted Annie Corsina Fox, an orphaned Catholic girl of seventeen, born in Australia and schooled in a Los Angeles convent. Her wealthy uncle and guardian, who considered the threadbare journeyman, then unemployed, an unacceptable suitor for her hand, ordered him from the house. This precipitated a crisis that led to the elopement of the two young people. The bridegroom was obliged to borrow not only the money for the wedding but even the clothes he wore to the occasion.

Not long after, George found work as a printer with a substantial Sacramento newspaper. This enabled him to pay his debts and even send money to his parents. But after some three years a disagreement with his foreman led to his discharge. Having lost his small savings in worthless mining stocks, he returned to San Francisco, followed shortly by his wife and infant firstborn son (future congressman Henry George, Jr.). The next thirteen months were to be a period of stark destitution; the job market was flooded with applicants, and George was unable to find steady work. He tried peddling clothes wringers and occasionally did substitute printing, then opened, with a friend, a modest printing shop that failed to yield sufficient income even for bare subsistence.

To feel the pinch of want when single had been bad enough; to be unable to provide for a growing family, infinitely worse. Annie, again pregnant, took in needlework to help pay the rent and pawned what little pieces of jewelry she had, until only her wedding ring (which had been her grandmother's) was left. The birth of their second child (Richard Fox George, who was to become a prominent sculptor) came at the very nadir of this time of hardship. Save for a loaf of bread a kindly neighbor had supplied, there was nothing in the house to eat. "Don't stop to wash the child," ordered the doctor. "The mother is starving—feed her!" Later that day, in a dismal rain, after stopping at the printing office to see if any customers had paid their bills, George went up to the first well-dressed man he met and asked him for five dollars, explaining that his wife was confined and needed food. Had the stranger not given him the money, George later recalled, "I think I was desperate enough to have killed him."

Although he was to experience financial uncertainty and debt for much of the remainder of his life, he would never again be faced with material circumstances so abysmal. Yet their memory was burned indelibly into his consciousness and played a signal role in directing him toward his eventual mission.

Budding Writer and Analyst

On April 15, 1865, word reached San Francisco of the assassination of President Lincoln. George had favored the abolitionist cause. So stirred was he by the tragic news that he wrote a brief but impassioned eulogy which he placed in the box of the editor of the *Alta California*, the city's oldest newspaper, at which he was then setting type. It was run as the lead editorial and, when the editor learned who its author was, he sought out George and gave him his earliest paid assignment as a writer. Newspapers began accepting his free-lance articles, and he became a reporter, editorial writer, and, at twenty-eight, managing editor of the San Francisco *Times*. Before long, he had exchanged this post for a similar one at the San Francisco *Chronicle*.

For four years George served as editor of his own daily, the San Francisco *Evening Post*. It was politically independent, and gained a wide and loyal readership through its vigorous exposure of corruption and misconduct. On more than one occasion, its editor exhibited physical as well as moral courage: confronting the pistol-wielding superintendent of a cruelly operated reform school; imposing a citizen's arrest upon a policeman who was mistreating an intoxicated man; being menaced with a revolver by a henchman of a police chief whose connivance with gambling interests he had brought to light; personally bringing successful suit against a ship captain and mate whose savage treatment had driven three shanghaied crewmen to suicide; and rescuing, at considerable peril to himself, a drunken sailor who was dangling by one hand from an iron balcony.

While George was working on the *Times*, his third child, Jane ("Jennie") Teresa, was born; she was to die prematurely as a young married woman, only a few months before her father. As a journalist, he had been giving deeper thought to social issues, discussing in editorials such topics as public franchises and subsidies, free trade, paper money, proportional representation, ballot reform, and women's rights. His article in the *Overland Monthly*, "What the Railroad Will Bring Us," dashed cold water on the popular enthusiasm for the linkage by rail of California to the East, and anticipated a theme that he would develop more profoundly in *Progress and Poverty*:

> The completion of the railroad and the consequent great increase of business and population will not be a benefit to all of us, but only to a portion. As a general rule (liable of course to exceptions) those who have, it will make wealthier; for those who have not it will make it more difficult to get. Those who have lands, mines, established business, special abilities of certain kinds, will become richer for it and find increased opportunities; those who have only their own labor will become poorer, and find it harder to get ahead.[2]

George was sent for half a year on newspaper business to New York City, which had become the premier metropolis of the Western Hemisphere. He was appalled by the obscene spectacle that it displayed of ostentatious luxury side by side with wretched squalor. There it was that, as he put it years later in a letter to an Irish priest, "in daylight, and in a city street, there came to me a thought, a vision, a call—give it what name you please. But every nerve quivered. And there and then I made a vow. Through evil and through good, whatever I have done and whatever I have left undone, to that I have been true."[3] His vow was to seek out and, if he could, remedy the cause that condemned people to debasing indigence in the midst of plenty.

A Flash, a Book, a Platform

Back in California, pondering on horseback the call to which he had responded in New York City, George experienced the moment of economic illumination that would set his future course:

> Absorbed in my own thoughts, I had driven the horse into the hills until he panted. Stopping for breath, I asked a passing teamster, for want of something better to say, what land was worth there. He pointed to some cows grazing off so far that they looked like mice and said: "I don't know exactly, but there is a man over there who will sell some land for a thousand dollars an acre." Like a flash it came upon me that there was the reason of advancing poverty with advancing wealth. With the growth of population, land grows in value, and the men who work it must pay more for the privilege. I turned

back, amidst quiet thought, to the perception that then came to me
and has been with me ever since.[4]

The following year, he wrote and published in small type a brief study,
Our Land and Land Policy, National and State, developing this insight and
setting forth his remedy in embryonic form. But he realized that to give
the subject the thorough treatment its importance warranted, a much larger
volume would be required.

On September 18, 1877, George entered the following notation in his
diary: "Commenced, 'Progress and Poverty.' " The following month saw the
birth of his last child, Anna Angela. She was to marry playwright William
de Mille and become the mother of Agnes de Mille, the well-known cho-
reographer.

The book's completion took a year and a half. When, in the dead of
night, George finished the last page, he flung himself to his knees, overcome
with powerful emotion, and wept like a babe, gratified that the talent
entrusted to him had been accounted for. He had fulfilled his vow. "The
rest," he said, "was in the Master's hands." He was then thirty-nine years
of age.

The work was unlike any other treatise on political economy. Unencum-
bered with dry statistics and mathematical jargon, its flowing cadences were
enlivened by quotations from poets and philosophers and even by Hindu
aphorisms, and the luminous clarity of its analysis was made vivid by pic-
turesque and homey illustrations from the author's own experience. It
approached its topic in both breadth and depth, leaving scarcely any aspect
of it unexplored, not stickling to include moral and spiritual arguments
along with purely economic ones in the assurance that "economic law and
moral law are essentially one."[5]

The book inquires as to why, in spite of the increase of productive power,
wages tend to the minimum of bare living; correlates the laws of distribution; locates the basic cause of industrial depressions; investigates the moral
nature and ground of property; proposes a practical solution to the problem, anticipating and answering most objections; and rises to a grand soci-
ological thesis as to the fall of civilizations and the formula for human
progress. Its chain of reasoning is carried forward with such charm and
force that Tolstoy expressed a sentiment widely held, in saying that "he
who becomes acquainted with it cannot but agree."[6] Of it, nearly seven
decades following its first publication, socially progressive prelate Dom Carlos Duarte Costa, bishop of Rio de Janeiro, was to declare: "After the
Gospel, this is the book that I love and admire the most."[7]

Initially it sold poorly while receiving, on the whole, respectable reviews.
It was issued in a cheaper paperback edition and translated into German.
Eventually the sale of *Progress and Poverty* picked up, and George was
enabled to realize an income by public lectures and by contributing articles
to major journals.

Nowhere in the Western world in those days was the land problem such a burning issue as in Ireland. Tenants in the Emerald Isle were ground down by rack rents and subjected to wholesale eviction by absentee landlords, largely English. Under the leadership of Charles Parnell and Michael Davitt, the Irish National Land League had been formed (with 2,500 American branches), and the fires of revolt were being stoked. On a visit to New York, Davitt met George and promised to promote *Progress and Poverty* in Ireland and Great Britain. George illustrated his general thesis about landownership in a small book, *The Irish Land Question*, which caused an immediate stir on both sides of the Atlantic. The New York *Irish World*, the foremost Irish-American newspaper, sent George to Ireland and Britain as a correspondent-lecturer. There he spoke to enthusiastic crowds and gained many influential friends, including two high ecclesiastics, Bishop Nulty of Meath and Bishop Duggan of Clonfert. He had the good fortune to be twice arrested and briefly jailed as a dangerous conspirator by British authorities in Galway, which made international news.

After a year abroad, George returned to find himself famous in his native land. *Progress and Poverty* had caught on in a big way. It would go into numerous editions and be translated into at least a dozen languages. By 1900 it had the greatest circulation of any nonfiction book in English, except for the Bible. This bore out his confidence in it, as expressed in a letter to his aged father accompanying the Author's Edition: "It will not be recognized at first—maybe not for some time—but it will ultimately be considered a great book, will be published in both hemispheres, and be translated into different languages."[8]

This statement reveals something about George's character. He was utterly unpretentious—simple and informal in dress, lifestyle, and demeanor—yet he had a proper sense of his own worth and never stooped to false humility. Although not by nature pugnacious, when matters of principle were at stake, he never temporized. He was quick to voice his indignation whenever he felt that he or others were unjustly put upon, which helps to explain why many of his jobs were of such short duration. Yet he was also quick to forgive; when he became managing editor of the *Chronicle*, he secured a post there for a printers' foreman who had once discharged him. Unlike most crusaders, he was a fun-loving man with a robust sense of humor who enjoyed playing harmless practical jokes but could also laugh at himself. He loathed all pretense and pomposity and had little reverence for wealth or station. However pressed with weighty matters, he was lavish with his time when it came to mending a child's broken doll, filling out a postal form for an illiterate stranger, or giving the benefit of his experience to a fledgling journalist or apprentice typographer.

In 1883, *Social Problems*, his second full-length book, was published. The next year he welcomed an invitation from the Land Reform Union to make a paid lecture tour of the United Kingdom. He normally spoke extemporaneously. When in his usual good form, he was an electrifying orator. His name was now a household word, and his addresses were hugely attended and given prominent attention in the press. George Bernard Shaw, who had chanced to hear him during his first transatlantic visit, was but one of myriads of that generation in the British Isles who, according to Shaw's biographer, were fired by the experience to enlist, in Heine's phrase, as soldiers in "the Liberative War of Humanity."[9] In many instances, however, including that of Shaw, their enlistment had results never intended by the speaker, for the social resolve that he awakened in them was later deflected toward collectivist schemes of which he strongly disapproved. Strenuous efforts were made to convert George himself to Marxism, but to no avail.

In Scotland, George found conditions even more appalling than in Ireland. He spoke outdoors to gatherings of impoverished crofters in the Highlands, and twice in the Glasgow city hall. After his first talk in that community, from whence his maternal grandfather had come, some five hundred persons stayed to organize the Scottish Land Restoration League. Two thousand enrolled in it after his second appearance, and branches were set up in Edinburgh, Dundee, Aberdeen, Inverness, and other communities.

Back in England, he lectured to a hostile and ill-mannered audience at Oxford University, but at Cambridge he was able to overcome initial opposition and carry the greater portion of his hearers with him at the end.

George then made a speaking tour in Canada under the auspices of the Knights of Labor, whose grand master, Terence V. Powderly, had had copies of *Progress and Poverty* placed in every local of his vast union. In 1886 George published another major work, *Protection or Free Trade*, on the tariff question.

First Mayoral Campaign

Although once a candidate for the California legislature, George no longer had ambition for public office as such, but thought of himself as one of those "who go in advance of politics . . . who break the road that after they have gone will be trod by millions."[10]

But now he was approached by a committee representing 165 labor unions with a total membership of fifty thousand, asking him to be their candidate for mayor of New York City. A platform reflecting his views was adopted by the newly formed United Labor Party. Prior to his formal nomination, an emissary came to him with a proposition from Tammany Hall (the corrupt machine that dominated city politics) and another Democratic Party faction. If he would withdraw from the race, which he had no chance of winning, they said, he could go to Europe or anywhere he chose and be guaranteed a certificate of election to the United States House of Representatives on his return.

"Why," he asked, "if I have no chance of winning, do you make this offer?"

"Because your running will raise hell," was the reply.

"You have relieved me of embarrassment," said George. "I do not want the responsibility and work of the office of the Mayor of New York, but I do want to 'raise hell!' I am decided and will run."[11]

Public supporters of George's candidacy represented widely varying positions. There were famous trade-union leaders such as Powderly of the Knights of Labor and Samuel Gompers of the American Federation of Labor. There were some sixty Protestant clergymen, ranging from Episcopalian to Universalist, and about forty Catholic priests. There were Felix Adler, founder of the Ethical Culture Society, and Robert Ingersoll, the "great agnostic." There were novelist William Dean Howells and painter George Inness. There were figures ranging from Robert C. Winthrop of Massachusetts' first family and a former Republican senator to Karl Marx's daughter, Eleanor, and her paramour, Dr. Edward Aveling.

For their candidate, the Democrats selected Abram S. Hewitt, a congressman for whom George had once done some ghost-writing and who now offered himself as the alternative to "anarchy and destruction." The Republicans chose a youthful former state assemblyman, Theodore Roosevelt, later to become president. The campaign was spirited and received worldwide publicity. After the balloting on November 3, 1886, the official tally placed Hewitt first, George second, Roosevelt last. That the returns had been manipulated against George was widely suspected. According to most historians, George was "voted in but counted out." As boss of Tammany, Richard Crocker admitted that they "could not allow a man like Henry George to be mayor" because "it would upset all their arrangements."[12]

George next launched a journal of social reconstruction, the weekly *Standard*. It stood for the taxation of land values alone, absolute free trade, and the Australian-model secret ballot. At first George took an active role as proprietor and principal writer. Gradually responsibilities were delegated to others. By the end of 1890 he transferred ownership and editorial control to a body of associates. Throughout its nearly six years of existence, the *Standard* lived up to its name, with its literate and thoughtful columns earning a reputation for exemplary advocacy journalism.

Although the Central Labor Union contained a strong socialist element, George never made any secret of his antipathy toward enforced collectivism. But the many members who also belonged to the Socialist Labor Party, a Marxist organization, attempted to commit the United Labor Party to its viewpoint. Instead, the United Labor Party expelled all who held membership in other parties. It was a reduced United Labor Party, therefore, that entered a full slate of candidates for all New York State offices open for election in 1887. Of these, the highest was that of secretary of state, to which George accepted nomination, much against his better judgment, and only out of a sense of duty to those who had stood with him in excluding the socialist contingent. The entire slate was crushingly defeated.

Run-in with the Church: The McGlynn Affair

The reasons for this poor showing go beyond the disaffection of the socialists. For one thing, the chief labor leaders, Powderly and Gompers, had come to favor withdrawal by their unions from direct partisan involvement. More importantly, George suffered a diminution of his Irish-American following as a result of the excommunication of his most active clerical adherent, Dr. Edward McGlynn.[13]

Father McGlynn, known as "the priest of the poor" and in many ways a precursor of this century's rebel priests of Latin America, had been rector of St. Stephen's, one of the largest and most important Roman Catholic parishes in the nation. Magnetic, independent, and fearless, he had already aroused suspicion in the hierarchy by his championship of public schools before he gave a rousing speech to support the nomination of George for mayor. In so doing he defied an order by his archbishop, Michael Corrigan, who was hand-in-glove with the New York power structure and regarded George's land theories (or rather, his distorted conception of them) as dangerously subversive.

Admonishing McGlynn to remain silent on political affairs, the archbishop and his vicar-general did not apply this advice to themselves. They publicly attacked George's ideas on land as "unsound, unsafe, and contrary to the teachings of the Church."[14] Although McGlynn had sought to keep a low profile so as to forestall dissension within the faith, he felt obliged to protest this slander in an interview in the New York *Tribune*. He was thereupon suspended from his priestly functions and summoned to the Vatican for an accounting. He declined to go, knowing the cards were stacked against him in the Office of the Propaganda of the Faith. His excommunication followed in due course, and priests who publicly expressed sympathy with him were abruptly transferred or demoted.

The incident became a *cause célèbre* and led a number of Catholics to abandon the Roman communion in disgust, much to McGlynn's dismay and against his repeated pleadings. On the other hand, many were cowed into dropping their support of George for fear they might themselves be excommunicated.

Deprived of ecclesiastical assignment, McGlynn made himself the main spark plug of the United Labor Party and, more than anyone else, was responsible for George's reluctant decision to lead its ill-starred slate.

McGlynn at this time also founded and became president of the Anti-Poverty Society. It held immense weekly meetings. The nucleus was his old parishioners, two of whom were later denied burial in consecrated ground as penalty for their attendance. At one of these meetings McGlynn delivered his famous address, "The Cross of the New Crusade" — a moving appeal for social Christianity based on the Creator's gift of nature for the use of all. George was vice president of the society and Hugh O. Pentecost, a prominent Congregationalist minister, one of its chief speakers. McGlynn and George certainly had no intention of establishing anything like a new denomination, but the Anti-Poverty Society had much in common with a church: Its meetings were held on Sunday evenings, the talks were biblical in emphasis and homiletical in presentation, music was directed by McGlynn's former choir leader, collection plates were passed, and the general atmosphere was evangelistic although theologically inclusive.

George's Religious Orientation

This raises the question of George's own religious views and associations. For a brief time during his youth, rebelling against the stifling and dogmatic piety in which he had been reared, he was a freethinker and, according to one biographer, an atheist.[15] When he was drawn back to Christianity just before he came of age, it was of a broader and more liberal stamp. But there came a time when, confronted by the spectacle of human misery on every hand and told by accepted theories of social science that grinding want for the many is an inescapable phenomenon built into the very structure of the universe, he was brought to a state of utter spiritual dessication.

In the course of fulfilling his great vow, however, he discovered that widespread involuntary poverty stems neither from the impersonal working of mechanistic natural forces nor from the arbitrary will of a cruel demiurge, but from man's deliberate flouting of divine fiat. "Out of this inquiry," he wrote in the concluding chapter of *Progress and Poverty*, "has come to me something I did not think to find, and a faith that was dead revives."

George eventually permitted his membership in the Methodist church to lapse and did not replace it with any other denominational affiliation. His wife, too, disassociated herself from any specific communion. Their children were baptized Catholics in deference to her sister, a nun of the Order of St. Vincent de Paul, and were allowed to make their own choice of religion. But this reflected no indifference to spiritual matters. Prayer, both morning and evening, was a regular feature of the family's life, and hymn singing was a frequent household practice. They cared nothing for liturgical forms or sectarian distinctions. The fatherhood of God, the brotherhood of man, the revelation of the divine beneficence in the person and work of Christ, and the continuation of individual life beyond the grave — these were the essentials of their highly ecumenical creed. It should be stressed that while George held strongly to the last of these as a constantly affirmed belief, he just as strongly castigated its degeneration into superstitious otherworldliness. Something of his thoughts in this regard may be gleaned from his most popular lecture, "Moses," first delivered in 1878 before the Young Men's Hebrew Association in San Francisco, and thereafter from pulpits throughout the English-speaking world:

> The continued existence of the soul, the judgment after death, the rewards and punishments of the future state, were the constant subjects of Egyptian thought and art. But . . . the doctrine of immortality, springing as it does from the very depths of human nature, ministering to aspirations which become stronger and stronger as intellectual life rises to higher planes and the life of the affections becomes more intense, may yet become so encrusted with degrading superstitions, may be turned by craft and selfishness into such a potent instrument for enslavement, so used to justify crimes at which every natural instinct revolts, that to the earnest spirit of the social reformer it may seem like an agency of oppression to enchain the intellect and prevent true progress; a lying device with which the cunning fetter the credulous.
>
> [The Hebrew religion] asserts not a God who is confined to the faroff beginning or the vague future, who is over and above and beyond all men, but a God who in His inexorable law is here and now; a God of the living as well as of the dead; a God of the marketplace as well as the temple; a God whose judgments wait not another world for execution, but whose immutable decrees will, in this life, give happiness to the people who heed them and bring misery upon the people who forget them.[16]

George's personal friends included clergy of nearly all persuasions, from Cardinal Henry Edward Manning to General and Mrs. William Booth of the Salvation Army. Those two great preachers of the Social Gospel, Washington Gladden and Walter Rauschenbusch, the one Congregationalist and the other Baptist, are emblematic of the many whose lives and thought he deeply touched. There was actually a body called the Single Tax Brotherhood of Religious Teachers, and even the miniscule Swedenborgian Church contained an active Georgist organization that published a monthly periodical of international circulation and must have contained a sizable proportion of that denomination's membership.

In Glasgow in 1889, during an extensive European speaking tour, he gave one of his outstanding talks, "Thy Kingdom Come," a passionate and powerful commentary on the Lord's Prayer. In London he engaged in polite debate with the Marxist H. M. Hyndman. His reception abroad and again on his return made it evident that the state election debacle had not significantly damaged his reputation. He then accepted an invitation to lecture in Australia, Annie George's native country. The two set off on what George called their "belated honeymoon" in January 1890. In San Francisco, where they boarded ship, he was honored by an enormous audience that paid to hear the former local typesetter, now world famous. A free meeting for working people was held later in the same hall, illustrating his characteristic willingness to speak for nothing or for a reduced honorarium, even though lecturing was a major source of his livelihood. The same with his books. In order to disseminate his message more widely, he sacrificed copyrights and royalties to such an extent that book sales, great though they were, brought him only a few hundred dollars a year.

The Georges stopped in New Zealand on their way to Sydney. They were entertained by the venerable Sir George Grey who, as prime minister, laid the groundwork for the considerable degree of land value taxation that his island commonwealth would adopt. Their three months in Australia were an uninterrupted triumph. George gave dozens of talks, always to packed and enthusiastic houses. As in New Zealand, many of his ideas found substantial lodgement and eventual enactment.

Back in America, George participated in the American Social Science Association's "Single Tax Debate." The most vehement attack on his position was by Edwin R. A. Seligman of Columbia University, a leading public-revenue specialist. The eloquent but acerbic exchange between the two was the high point of the proceedings. Seligman, with his Ph.D. and law degree, condemned George as a well-meaning but naïve and ignorant fanatic who presumed to set himself up as an authority on arcane topics better left to properly certified experts.

As a matter of fact, it was George's misfortune to launch his theory just as economics was becoming a specialized profession. Scholars in this discipline, as distinct from scholars in general, often regarded him with patronizing coolness because of his lack of educational credentials. Many were put off, also, by characteristics that seemed unprofessional to them — characteristics suggested by the terms "theologian," "reformer," "social revolutionist" and "Christian activist."

The verdict half a century later was quite different, when the magisterial Joseph Schumpeter said of George: "He was a self-taught economist, but he *was* an economist. In the course of his life, he acquired most of the knowledge and the ability to handle an economic argument that he could have acquired by academic training as it then was."[17] John Bates Clark, the other college economist who participated in the debate on the opposition side, came to be honored for his theory of marginal productivity (advanced nine years after the famous debate). Clark was fair and magnanimous enough to explicitly acknowledge his debt to George for the idea from which this theory was developed.[18]

The strain of unremitting speaking and writing took its toll. George was stricken with a slight brain hemorrhage which resulted in temporary aphasia — loss of the power to express himself orally. The condition lasted only a few days, but his doctors gave him stern orders to rest. Fortunately, two well-to-do disciples arranged for him and Annie to convalesce in Bermuda. One was Tom L. Johnson, who was beginning an illustrious political career as Ohio congressman and reform mayor of Cleveland. The other was

August Lewis, a New York importer and manufacturer.

Without being asked, these admirers and benefactors also took it on themselves to relieve George from financial pressure so he could devote himself to a definitive and comprehensive text that he had proposed to write. George wanted to reinforce the principles stated in *Progress and Poverty* in a broader scholastic framework, delving into such economic topics as value, money, and banking. As it turned out, interruptions unrelated to pecuniary problems left this effort incomplete, even though the posthumously published work, *The Science of Political Economy*, runs to more than five hundred pages.

Confronting the Pope

In 1891 Pope Leo XIII issued his encyclical, *Rerum Novarum*, which has become a fundamental document of modern Catholic economic policy. It contains certain statements which George took to be express condemnations of his proposals. Although he was probably mistaken in this, his belief was not unreasonable, for the passages are worded in a way that is susceptible of that interpretation. Archbishop Corrigan read them the same way, taking them as a vindication of his position.

George applied the next five months to preparing his reply, *The Condition of Labor, an Open Letter to Pope Leo XIII*, published as a short book.[19] It was an eloquent work. George essayed to distinguish his teaching from anarchism on the one hand and socialism on the other, and to show that it in no wise contradicted Church doctrine. The *Open Letter* addresses Leo in respectful and even reverent tone, emphasizing the shared natural law assumptions on which his and George's social views are based. It applauds the "many wholesome truths" in the encyclical and pays tribute to Leo's "desire to help the suffering and oppressed." Yet it audaciously but courteously ventures to correct the pontiff's misconstruction of George's theory and the inadequacy of programs advocated in the papal document. A copy of the Italian edition was put into Leo's hands via the Vatican Library, but George never received (or expected) any direct acknowledgment.

George surmised that he received an indirect acknowledgment the following year, however, as he reported to his friend, Father Thomas Dawson:

> Something wonderful has happened on this side of the water. The Pope has quietly but effectively sat down on the ultramontane toryism of prelates like Archbishop Corrigan. ... Dr. McGlynn is to be restored, and the fighting of the Single Tax as opposed to Catholicism effectually ended. I have for some time believed Leo XIII to be a very great man, but this transcends my anticipations. Whether he ever read my "Letter" I cannot tell, but he has been acting as though he had not only read it, but had recognized its force.[20]

Archbishop Francesco Satolli, a theologian who belonged to Leo's inner circle, had come to the United States as papal representative. Satolli personally investigated McGlynn's case and invited him to submit a statement of the beliefs that had led to his excommunication. His memorandum, consisting largely of passages from George's writing, was subjected to the scrutiny of a panel of four experts from Catholic University, who attested unanimously that it contained nothing contrary to doctrine.

On Christmas Eve, much to Corrigan's displeasure, the excommunication was unconditionally reversed and McGlynn reinstated in his priestly functions.[21] Next spring McGlynn went to Rome and received the pope's blessing in a half-hour private audience. Interestingly, three years earlier, George's works were secretly condemned by the Inquisition but never officially placed on the Index of Forbidden Books. Concurrent with McGlynn's reinstatement, George's books were treated as "free doctrine" — meaning Catholics may accept or reject them according to their individual convictions.

Second Campaign — End of a Life

George was entreated in 1897 by an alliance of anti-Tammany Democrats to run again, this time on an independent ticket, for mayor of America's largest city. He was reluctant to accept the bid, since he knew this might preclude the completion of his political economy treatise. Besides, four physicians warned that he could either continue to write and live — or run for mayor and die. They said his constitution would not stand the strain of another political contest.

He called a meeting of some thirty friends, asking their advice with the proviso they make no reference to his physical condition. When they finished, he summarized, pointing out that each had admitted his candidacy would publicize the principles in which they all believed. He concluded, therefore, that it was his clear duty to accept the nomination.

George named his independent party "The Democracy of Thomas Jefferson." His main opponent was the front man for the Tammany machine, Judge Robert A. Van Wyck, handpicked by its boss, Crocker. The regular Republicans put up a former secretary of the navy, General Benjamin F. Tracy. The Citizens Union, made up of reform Republicans, nominated Seth Low, president of Columbia University.

George's younger daughter, just turned twenty, heard his acceptance speech at an overflow meeting on October 5. She recalled how frail and ashen he appeared, saying his voice at first was weak, almost inaudible. But gradually it rose to something like its old resonance:

The office for which you name me gives me no power to carry out in full my views, but I can represent those who think with me . . . that all men are created free and equal. . . . No greater honor can be given to any man than to stand for that. . . . No greater service can he render to his day and generation than to lay at its feet whatever he has. I would not refuse it if I died for it. What counts a few years? What can a man do better or nobler than something for his country, for his nation, for his age?[22]

His entry focused international attention on the race, and distinguished supporters from points as distant as San Francisco came to New York to lend their help. There was mutual respect and even some cooperation between George and Low, who was actually elected mayor four years later. It was hinted George might throw his support to Low in a merger of reform forces, but these hints were belied by his statement about Low: "He is a Republican and he is fighting the machine, which is all very good as far as it goes. But he is an aristocratic reformer; I am a democratic reformer. He would help the people; I would help the people to help themselves."[23]

The contest seemed at first to bring new strength and zest to the enfeebled warrior. But it was soon apparent he was driving himself beyond his limit. He set a grueling schedule that outpaced all three of his opponents. He made thirty speeches in the last twelve days, insisting, even when almost prostrate with exhaustion, upon addressing every audience that had gathered to hear him.

On the night of his death he spoke four times. At College Point, where he appeared before a mass assemblage of workingmen, he was introduced as a great friend of labor. George, who had been a union member all his adult life and who had twice run as standard-bearer of the United Labor Party, responded with his famous blunt independence: "I have never claimed to be a special friend of labor. Let us have done with this call for special privileges for labor. I have never asked for special rights or sympathy for working men! What I stand for is the equal rights of all men."[24]

At the Union Square Hotel, where he stayed during the campaign, George and his wife had a late supper with six friends. Before going to bed after one in the morning, he complained of indigestion. Toward daybreak, his wife found him standing rigid as a statue, his face white, repeating as if to an invisible presence the word "Yes." Soon afterward, he lapsed into unconsciousness, felled fatally by a massive stroke. It was less than five days before the election.

His body was carried to the Grand Central Palace. It was accompanied, Roman-style, by the fine bronze bust his sculptor son, Richard, had made of him earlier in the year. From seven in the morning until two in the afternoon, when the doors were shut, as many as 100,000 mourners passed his bier. At the funeral service, four clergy of different faiths—Episcopalian, Congregationalist, Jewish, and Roman Catholic—delivered eulogies. The last of these, Father McGlynn, called forth spontaneous applause, unprecedented for an occasion of such solemnity, when he said:

He was not merely a philosopher and sage; he was a seer, a forerunner, a prophet; a teacher sent from God. And we can say of him as the Scriptures say: "There was a man sent of God whose name was John." And I believe I mock not those Scriptures when I say: There was a man sent from God whose name was Henry George![25]

Notes

CHAPTER 1

1. Susan George, *How the Other Half Dies* (New York: Penguin Books, 1976), 24. We have seen nothing to indicate that these statistics have changed significantly. (One hectare = 2.47 acres.)

2. Onora O'Neill, *Faces of Hunger* (London: Allen & Unwin, 1986). Economists Sergio Molina and Sebastian Pinera calculated that in 1970 approximately 40 percent of all Latin Americans received an income below $200 per year (paper for the Catholic Social Action Center of Latin America, 1978). On the difficulties of calculating poverty, *see* A. J. M. Hagenaars, *The Perception of Poverty* (Amsterdam: Elsevier Science Publishers, 1986).

3. The terms "monopolist" and "monopoly," applied to land, are used throughout this book in the broad sense typical of classical economics tradition. Many contemporary economists decline to interpret land rent as a monopoly price because "as long as land has alternative uses and many owners it comes to be supplied under conditions approaching competition." (Robert F. Hébert, in R. V. Andelson, ed., *Critics of Henry George* [Rutherford, N.J.: Fairleigh Dickinson University Press, 1979], 63). But in much of the world, the ownership of land is concentrated under the control of so small a minority that any term other than monopoly, even in the strict contemporary sense, would be inappropriate. Moreover, within given locations the supply of land is inelastic; so even where its ownership is diffuse, land rent still involves an intrinsically *monopolistic element*. While alternative uses of land may soften the monopoly effect in some cases, the inherent limitations of a supply fixed by nature gives the owner of land a built-in advantage over nonowners.

4. *See,* for example, Deut. 4:43; Josh. 16:61; 20:8; 1 Kings 9:18; 1 Chron. 6:78; 2 Chron. 8:4; Ps. 65:12.

5. Andre Gunder Frank contends that a greater share of the profit in Latin America since World War II has gone to outside interests. He admits that industrial growth rose from 11 percent of the gross domestic product in 1925 to 23 percent in 1967, but claims that industrial employment remained at a constant 14 percent of the total labor force. He found that per capita incomes grew at a rate of 4.8 percent per year from 1945 through 1949, but grew at only 1.2 percent annually from 1960 through 1966. *See* Frank, *Lumpenbourgeoisie: Lumpendevelopment*, trans. Marion Davis Berdecio (New York and London: Monthly Review Press, 1972), chapter 8.

6. Deane William Ferm, ed., *Third World Liberation Theologies: An Introductory Survey* (Maryknoll, N.Y.: Orbis Books, 1986), p. 6.

7. This is not to say, of course, that materialism is not rife among the denizens of the Third World, too, or that some of the criticism of North American and

European materialism may not stem from envy and *ressentiment*. Mere failure to amass material goods is scarcely in itself a proof of spirituality.

8. Franz Hinkelammert, *Las Armas Ideológicas de la Muerte* (San José, Costa Rica: Departamento Ecuménico de Investigaciones, 1981). English translation, *The Ideological Weapons of Death: A Theological Critique of Capitalism*, trans. Phillip Berryman (Maryknoll, N.Y.: Orbis Books, 1986). *See also* H. Assmann, F. Hinkelammert, P. Richard, et al., *A luta dos deuses. Os ídolos da opressão e a busca do Deus Libertador* (São Paulo: Edições Paulinas, 1982).

9. Marcelo de Barros Souza, *A Bíblia e a luta pela terra*, 2d ed. (Petrópolis, Brazil: Vozes, 1983).

10. Marcelo de Barros Souza, *Nossos pais nos contaram* (Petrópolis, Brazil: Vozes, 1984).

11. For information in English concerning the Basic Ecclesial Communities, *see* Marcelo de Azevedo, *Basic Ecclesial Communities in Brazil* (Washington, D.C.: Georgetown University Press, 1986). *See also* the article by the same author, "Basic Ecclesial Communities: A Meeting Point of Ecclesiologies," *Journal of Theological Studies* 46 (1985), 601–20; Alvaro Barreiro, *Basic Ecclesial Communities: The Evangelization of the Poor*, trans. Barbara Campbell (Maryknoll, N.Y.: Orbis Books, 1982); and John Eagleson and Sergio Torres, eds., *The Challenge of Basic Christian Communities* (Maryknoll, N.Y.: Orbis Books, 1981).

12. For a description of how the Bible is used in these communities, *see* two books by Carlos Mesters: *Flor Sem Defesa* (Petrópolis: Vozes, 1983). English translation, *Defenseless Flower: A New Reading of the Bible*, trans. F. McDonagh (Maryknoll, N.Y.: Orbis Books, 1989) and *Por Trás das Palavras* (Petrópolis: Vozes, 1984).

13. Charles Avila, *Ownership: Early Christian Teaching* (Maryknoll, N.Y.: Orbis Books, 1983).

14. Ibid., 53.

15. Ibid.

16. Quoted in ibid., 62.

17. Quoted in ibid., 94, 132.

18. Ibid., 96–97.

19. Ibid., 114.

20. Ibid., 123.

21. *Summa Theologica* 2a2ae, 32.6

22. *Acta Apostolicae Sedis* (1941), 199.

23. *Mater et Magistra*, Part I, art. 43.

24. R. V. Andelson, *Imputed Rights: An Essay in Christian Social Theory* (Athens, Ga.: University of Georgia Press, 1971).

25. Henry George, *Progress and Poverty*, first published in 1879, remains an all-time bestseller on economic theory and policy. (New York: Robert Schalkenbach Foundation, 1970).

26. Alex Shoumatoff, *The World Is Burning: Murder in the Rain Forest* (Boston: Little, Brown and Company, 1990), 79.

27. Ibid., 66.

28. Ibid., 89.

29. Ibid., 117–21.

30. Henry George, *Protection or Free Trade* (New York: Robert Schalkenbach Foundation, 1980).

31. Gerard Elfstrom, *Moral Issues and Multinational Corporations* (London and New York: Macmillan and St. Martin's Press, 1991), 6.

32. Ibid., 115f.

33. R. V. Andelson, ed., *Commons Without Tragedy: Protecting the Environment from Overpopulation — a New Approach* (London and New York: Shepheard-Walwyn and Barnes & Noble, 1991), chapter 2.

CHAPTER 2

1. *See* Leonardo Boff, *Paixão de Christo Paixão do Mundo* (Petrópolis: Vozes, 1977). English translation, *Passion of Christ, Passion of the World: The Facts, Their Interpretation and Their Meaning Yesterday to Today*, trans. R. Barr (Maryknoll, N.Y.: Orbis Books, 1987).

2. The Treaty of Tordesillas, established between Castile and Portugal on June 7, 1494, set a line of demarcation 370 leagues west of the Cape Verde Islands, between 48° and 49° west of Greenwich. For some of the social consequences of this treaty, *see* James Lockhart and Stuart B. Schwartz, *Early Latin America* (London: Cambridge University Press, 1983), 64, 184–85, 203.

3. Lyle N. McAlister, *Spain and Portugal in the New World, 1492–1700* (Minneapolis: University of Minnesota Press, 1984), 153–81. Celso Furtado, *Economic Development of Latin America: A Survey from Colonial Times to the Cuban Revolution* (London: Cambridge University Press, 1971), 29–31, 125–26.

4. Furtado, *Economic Development*, 29.

5. In the Papal Bull of 1537, Paul III declared the Indians to be "real men." The early churchman who was most responsive to the needs of the Indians was Bartolome de Las Casas. For the Roman Catholic Church's general attitude toward Indians and landowners, *see* Nicholas P. Cushner, *Lords of the Land* (Albany, N.Y.: SUNY Press, 1980).

6. Robert G. Keith, ed., *Haciendas and Plantations in Latin American History* (New York and London: Holmes & Meier, 1977); C. Furtado, *Economic Growth of Brazil, A Survey from Colonial to Modern Times* (Berkeley, Calif.: University of California Press, 1963).

7. Michael Redclift, *Development and the Environmental Crisis: Red or Green Alternatives?* (London, New York: Methuen, 1984), 71.

8. Maria Vargas-Lobsinger, *La Hacienda de "La Concha": Una Empresa Algodonera de la Laguna, 1883–1917* (Mexico: Universidad Nacional Autonoma de Mexico, 1984), 109–26; A. W. Johnson, *Sharecroppers of the Sertão: Economics and Dependence on a Brazilian Plantation* (Cambridge, Mass.: Harvard University Press, 1971); Nino S. Sepulveda, *El atraso rural colombiano* (Bogotá: Editorial El Catolicismo, 1979); R. Stavenhagen, ed., *Agrarian Problems and Peasant Movements in Latin America* (New York: Doubleday, Anchor Books, 1970).

9. *See* Furtado, *Economic Development*, 71–80. Joseph S. Tulchin, *Problems in Latin American History: The Modern Period* (New York: Harper & Row, 1973), 40; M. Sternberg, "The Latifundista: The Impact of His Income and Expenditure Patterns on Income and Consumption," *Studies in Comparative International Development* 7 (1972), 1–18.

10. J. V. Levin, *The Export Economies: Their Pattern of Development in Historical Perspective* (Cambridge, Mass.: Harvard University Press, 1960); E. J. Mishan, *The Costs of Economic Growth* (London: Staples Press, 1967).

11. Alan Gilbert, *Latin American Development* (Harmondsworth, Middlesex: Penguin Books Ltd., 1974), 139; R. C. Young, "The Plantation Economy and Industrial Development in Latin America," *Economic Development and Cultural Change* 18 (1970), 342–61; W. C. Thiesenhusen, "A Suggested Policy for Industrial Reinvigoration in Latin America," *Journal of Latin American Studies* 4 (1972), 85–104.

12. James E. Austin, *Agribusiness in Latin America* (New York and London: Praeger, 1974).

13. Eduardo Galeano, *Open Veins of Latin America: Five Centuries of the Pillage of a Continent*, trans. C. Belfrage (New York: Monthly Review Press, 1973).

14. D. J. Robinson, "Venezuela and Colombia," in H. Blakemore and C. T. Smith, *Latin America: Geographical Perspectives* (London: Methuen and Co. Ltd., 1974), 179–246; D. W. Adams, "Land Ownership Patterns in Colombia," *Inter-American Economic Affairs* 17 (1964), 77–86; "Colombia's Land Tenure System: Antecedents and Problems," *Land Economics* 42 (1966), 43–53; "Rural Migration and Agricultural Development in Colombia," *Economic Development and Cultural Change* 17 (1969), 527–39; E. A. Duff, "Agrarian Reforms in Colombia. Problems of Social Reform," *Journal of Inter-American Studies* 8 (1966), 75–88.

15. Andre Gunder Frank, *On Capitalist Underdevelopment* (New York: Oxford University Press, 1975), 260.

CHAPTER 3

1. Ecuador is an exception in that it seeks foreign investment in its oil industry.

2. For a biography of Simon Patino, *see* Charles Geddes, *Patino: The Tin King* (London: Robert Hale, 1972).

3. Jan Bazant, *Alienation of Church Wealth in Mexico: Social and Economic Aspects of the Liberal Revolution, 1856–1875* (London: Cambridge University Press, 1970).

4. R. Stavenhagen, "Social Aspects of Agrarian Structure in Mexico," in R. Stavenhagen, ed., *Agrarian Problems*, 225–70; F. R. Brandenburg, *The Making of Modern Mexico* (Englewood Cliffs, N.J.: Prentice-Hall, 1964); Furtado, *Economic Development*, 74, 254–264.

5. D. Henderson, "Arid lands under agrarian reform in northwest Mexico," *Economic Geography* 41 (1965), 300–12; R. S. Weckstein, "Evaluating Mexican Land Reform," *Economic Development and Cultural Change* 18 (1970), 391–409; Gerardo Otero, "Agrarian Reform in Mexico: Capitalism and the State," in William C. Thiesenhusen, ed., *Searching for Agrarian Reform in Latin America* (Boston: Unwin Hyman, 1989), 276–304.

6. V. J. Fifer, *Bolivia: Land, Location and Politics since 1825* (London: Cambridge University Press, 1972); E. Flores, "Land Reform in Bolivia," *Land Economics* 30 (1954), 112–24; Mocayo J. Flores, "Bases of the Agrarian Reform in Bolivia," in T. L. Smith, ed., *Agrarian Reform in Latin America* (New York: Alfred Knopf, 1965), 120–28; D. B. Heath, "Land Reform in Bolivia," *Inter-American Economic Affairs* 12 (1959), 3–27; D. B. Heath, C. J. Erasmus, and H. C. Buechler, *Land Reform and Social Revolution in Bolivia* (New York: Praeger, 1968); C.H. Zondag, *The Bolivian Economy, 1952–1965: The Revolution and Its Consequences* (New York: Praeger, 1966).

7. Sven Lindqvist, *Land and Power in South America*, trans. Paul Britten Austin (Harmondsworth, Middlesex: Penguin Books Ltd., 1979), 275.

8. Ibid., 286–87.

9. Rosemary Thorp and Geoffrey Bertram, *Peru 1890–1977* (New York: Columbia University Press, 1978); Trelles W. Zuniga, *Peru: agricultura, reforma agraria y desarrollo economico* (Lima: Editorial Imprenta Amauta, 1970).

10. D. Olden, "The Spatial Distribution of Population in Relation to Wealth and Welfare in Colombia, Mexico and Peru" (University of London: M. Phil. thesis, 1971); A. Quijano, *Nationalism and Capitalism in Peru: A Study in Neo-Imperialism* (New York: Monthly Review Press, 1971).

11. S. Aranda, *La revolucion agraria en Cuba* (Mexico: Siglo XXI Editores S. A., 1968); D. Barkin, "Cuban Agriculture: A Strategy of Economic Development," *Studies in Comparative International Development* 6 (1972a), 19–38; H. Thomas, *Cuba: Or the Pursuit of Freedom* (London: Eyre and Spottiswoode, 1971).

12. *Emphyteusis*, in ancient Roman law, denoted a perpetual lease of lands and tenements in consideration of annual rent and of improvements. In many ways this law prefigured the advanced conception of land reform that is set forth later in this work.

13. C. Villalobos-Dominguez, "Argentina," in Harry Gunnison Brown, Harold S. Buttenheim, Philip H. Cornick, and Glenn E. Hoover, eds., *Land-Value Taxation Around the World* (New York: Robert Schalkenbach Foundation, 1955), 166.

14. Lindqvist, *Land and Power in South America*, 292–97.

15. Saul Trinidad and Juan Stam, "Christ in Latin American Protestant Preaching," in José Míguez Bonino, ed., *Faces of Jesus*, trans. Robert R. Barr (Maryknoll, N.Y.: Orbis Books, 1984), 39–48.

16. *See* Diana D. Brown, *Umbanda: Religion and Politics in Urban Brazil* (Ann Arbor, Mich.: UMI Research Press, 1986).

17. *See* Gerhard Kittel, ed., *Theological Dictionary of the New Testament* I, trans. G. W. Bromiley (Grand Rapids, Mich.: Eerdmans, 1972), 564–93.

18. Walter Brueggemann, *The Land: Place as Gift, Promise, and Challenge in Biblical Faith* (Philadelphia: Fortress Press, 1977).

19. *Quadragesimo Anno*, arts. 57–58, in *Seven Great Encyclicals* (Glen Rock, N.J.: Paulist Press, 1963), 141f.

20. *See*, for example, Leo XIII's encyclical, *Rerum Novarum* (Official English version, Vatican Polyglot Press, May 15, 1891).

CHAPTER 4

1. Leonardo Boff, *Church: Charism and Power*, trans. John W. Diercksmeier (New York: Crossroad Publishing Company, 1985), 2–7.

2. A good introduction to Augustine's ideas of Church and society is Herbert A. Deane, *The Political and Social Ideas of St. Augustine* (New York and London: Columbia University Press, 1963). *See also* Robert A. Markus, " 'De Civitate Dei', XIX, 14–15 and the Origins of Political Authority" in *Saeculum: History and Society in the Theology of St. Augustine* (Cambridge, England: Cambridge University Press, 1970), 197–210.

3. Boff, *Church: Charism and Power*, 2–3.

4. The role of Freemasonry in this context is worth passing mention. For expositions of this influence in Cuba and Mexico, *see* Fernando Ortiz, *Momento Actual de America* (Matanzas, Cuba: Gaylamount, 1948) and Felix Navarrete, *La Masoneria en La História y en las Leyes de Mejico*, 2d ed. (Mexico: Editorial Jus, 1962).

5. Boff, *Church: Charism and Power*, 5.

6. Ibid., 5–6.

7. This emphasis, it will be recognized, has also characterized some aspects of the Reformed tradition in Protestantism.

8. Boff, *Church: Charism and Power*, 7.

9. Ibid., 9.

10. This is the underlying concern of Xabier Pikaza, *Anunciar a Liberdade aos Cativos*, trans. L. J. Gaio (São Paulo: Edições Loyola, 1985), especially 404–406. For a more popular example, *see* Dom Helder Camara, *The Desert Is Fertile*, trans. F. McDonagh (Maryknoll, N.Y.: Orbis Books, 1981).

11. Because sin and salvation are *corporate* terms in much of the Bible, liberation theologians insist that God reveals himself to a *people* in a particular historic context.

12. *See* J. Severino Croatto, *Liberacion y libertad: Pautas hermenêuticas* (Lima: CEP, 1978); *Biblical Hermeneutics: Toward a Theory of Reading as the Production of Meaning*, trans. R. Barr (Maryknoll, N.Y.: Orbis Books, 1987); Marcelo de Barros Souza, *Nossos pais nos contaram*; Carlos Mesters, *Palavra de Deus na História dos Homens* 1 (Petrópolis: Vozes, 1984); *Por Trás das Palavras*; *Defenseless Flower: A New Reading of the Bible*.

13. Our italics.

14. *See* Juan Luis Segundo, *Jesus of Nazareth Yesterday and Today*, vol. 1, trans. J. Drury (Maryknoll, N.Y.: Orbis Books, 1984).

15. The literature on Baalism is extensive. For surveys, *see* the bibliographies appended to J. Gray, "Baal (Deity)," in G. A. Butrick, ed., *The Interpreter's Dictionary of the Bible* I (Nashville and New York: Abingdon Press, 1962), 328–329; M. H. Pope, "Mot," in Keith Crim, ed., *The Interpreter's Dictionary of the Bible* (Nashville, Tenn.: Abingdon, 1976), supplement, 607–608.

16. Gerhard von Rad, *The Message of the Prophets*, trans. D. M. G. Stalker (New York: Harper & Row, 1967), 110–17. For a commentary on specific passages, *see* James Luther Mays, *Hosea* (Philadelphia: Westminster Press, 1969).

17. Quoted by Robert L. Heilbroner, *The Worldly Philosophers*, 5th ed. (New York: Simon and Schuster, 1980), 80.

18. Henry George, *Progress and Poverty*, 295.

CHAPTER 5

1. Leonardo Boff, *Church: Charism and Power*, 24–25; R. E. Brown, "The Beatitudes according to St. Luke," in *New Testament Essays* (Garden City, N.Y.: Image Books, 1965), 334–41; Joseph A. Fitzmyer, *The Gospel According to Luke*, I–IX (Garden City, N.Y.: Doubleday & Company, Inc., 1982), 625–46.

2. Robert C. Tannehill reminds us that in Luke "in a variety of ways Jesus speaks of 'fruit' as the crucial test for individuals and people (6:43–44; 8:8, 15; 20:10), and he echoes John's warning that the tree which does not bear fruit for its owner will be chopped down (13:6–9). Jesus (6:30, 34–35), like John (3:10–11), requires sharing of goods with others, and Jesus applies John's warning when he describes the fate of one who calls 'Abraham as father' but has not produced 'fruit worthy of repentance' through sharing with the poor (16:19–31; cf. 3:8)." *The Narrative Unity of Luke Acts* I (Philadelphia: Fortress Press, 1986), 145.

3. Gustavo Gutiérrez, *The Power of the Poor in History*, trans. Robert R. Barr (Maryknoll, N.Y.: Orbis Books, 1983).

4. Gerhard Friedrich, ed., *Theological Dictionary of the New Testament* II, trans. G. W. Bromiley (Grand Rapids, Mich.: Eerdmans, 1968), 477–85.

5. *See* Krister Stendahl, "Judgment and Mercy," in *Paul Among Jews and Gentiles* (Philadelphia: Fortress Press, 1976), 97–108.

6. Gustavo Gutiérrez, "Expanding the View," in Marc H. Ellis and Otto Maduro, eds., *Expanding the View: Gustavo Gutiérrez and the Future of Liberation Theology* (Maryknoll, N.Y.: Orbis Books, 1990), 12.

7. John Rawls has likened justice to a system of social insurance that people ignorant of their future circumstances might be expected to choose prudentially — to protect against bad luck. John Rawls, *A Theory of Justice* (Cambridge, Mass.: The Belknap Press of Harvard University Press, 1971). This is a position that one of the present writers has disputed. Robert V. Andelson, "Vive la Difference? Rawls' 'Difference Principle' and the Fatal Premise upon Which It Rests," *The Personalist* 56: 2 (Spring, 1975), 207–13. Here it should suffice to point out that Rawls's view is not the biblical position.

8. Edwin Markham, "The Man With the Hoe," in Louis Untermayer, ed., *Modern American Poetry* (New York: Harcourt, Brace and Company, 1921), 49.

9. Nicolas Berdyaev, *Christianity and Class War* (1931), trans. Donald Attwater (New York: Sheed & Ward, 1933), 17.

10. Gustavo Gutiérrez, *The Power of the Poor in History*; Gutiérrez, *Teologia da Libertação*, trans. Jorge Soares, 2d ed. (Petrópolis: Vozes, 1976), 235–49; Leonardo Boff, *A Fé Na Periferia do Mundo*, 2d ed. (Petrópolis: Vozes, 1979), especially 57–75. English translation, *Faith on the Edge: Religion and Marginalized Existence* (Maryknoll, N.Y.: Orbis Books, 1991).

11. Fyodor Dostoyevsky, *The Brothers Karamazov*, trans. Constance Garnette (New York: Modern Library, 1950), 294–309.

12. Nicolas Berdyaev, *The Destiny of Man* (1931), trans. Natalie Duddington (New York: Harper Torchbooks, 1960), 100f.

13. Jon Sobrino, *Resurrección de la verdadera Iglesia: Los pobres, lugar teológico de la eclesiología* (Santander, Spain: Editorial Sal Terrae, 1981). English translation, *The True Church and the Poor*, trans. M. O'Connell (Maryknoll, N.Y.: Orbis Books, 1984).

14. Whatever may be the case with Sobrino and others, when the present authors speak of "the Church," they are not necessarily referring to any ecclesiastical institution issuing pronouncements in an official capacity but simply to the body of those who look to Christ as their Redeemer and Exemplar.

CHAPTER 6

1. *See* Rubem A. Alves, *A Theology of Human Hope* (St. Meinrad, Ind.: Abbey Press, 1975), 27–68.

2. *See* Reinhold Niebuhr, *Moral Man and Immoral Society* (New York: Scribners, 1932).

3. *Populorum Progressio*, arts. 1–31.

4. Ibid., art. 14.

5. Ibid., arts. 23–24.

6. Ibid.

7. Ibid., arts. 26, 30–31.

8. Ibid., arts. 57–58, 78.

9. Gustavo Gutiérrez, *Teologia de la Liberacion* (Salamanca: Ediciones Sigumeme, 1972). English translation, *A Theology of Liberation*, trans. and ed. Sister Caridad Inda and John Eagleson (Maryknoll, N.Y.: Orbis Books, 1973).

10. Gutiérrez, *A Theology of Liberation*, 29, 79.

11. Ibid., 25–28.

12. Ibid.

13. For a compendium of esoteric controversies between dependency theorists and Marxists, and among Marxists concerning the relationship of dependency theory to Marxism, *see* Ronald H. Chilcote, ed., *Dependency and Marxism: Toward a Resolution of the Debate* (Boulder, Colo.: Westview Press, 1982).

14. Ibid., 87.

15. Gustavo Gutiérrez, *The Power of the Poor in History*; "Teologia y ciencias Sociales," *Christus*, October–November, 1984.

16. Gutiérrez, "Expanding the View," 10.

17. Leonardo Boff, *Liberating Grace*, trans. John Drury (Maryknoll, N.Y.: Orbis Books, 1979), 65.

18. Arthur F. McGovern, "Dependency Theory, Marxist Analysis, and Liberation Theology," in Ellis and Maduro, eds., *Expanding the View*, 85. McGovern's fuller assessment of liberation theology is found in *Liberation Theology and Its Critics: Toward an Assessment* (Maryknoll, N.Y.: Orbis Books, 1989).

19. Remarks expressed in conversation with one of the present authors by Rubem Alves, Campinas, Brazil, August 12, 1985.

20. Henry George, *Protection or Free Trade* (New York: Robert Schalkenbach Foundation, 1980).

21. Gutiérrez, "Expanding the View," 10; Boff, *Liberating Grace*, 65.

22. Joseph Ramos, "Dependency and Development" and "Latin America: The End of Democratic Reformism" in Michael Novak, ed., *Liberation South/Liberation North* (Washington, D.C.: American Institute for Public Policy Research, 1981), 62f., 74–77.

23. Sergio Molina and Sebastian Pinera, "Extreme Poverty in Latin America" in Novak, *Liberation South/Liberation North*, 85.

24. Ramos, "Dependency and Development," in Novak, *Liberation South/Liberation North*, 61.

25. Michael Novak, *Will It Liberate?* (New York: Paulist Press, 1986), 56, 85–92.

26. Gutiérrez, "Expanding the View," 10.

27. Novak, *Will It Liberate?* 60, 75, 79, 92, 130, 134, 136, 138–40, 149.

28. Andre Gunder Frank, *Capitalism and Underdevelopment in Latin America* (New York: Monthly Review Press, 1967), 211f.

29. David Richards, "Missing Links in the New Economics," *Land and Liberty* (March-April 1987), 20.

CHAPTER 7

1. José Comblin, *The Church and the National Security State* (Maryknoll, N.Y.: Orbis Books, 1979), 66, 132, 140–42, 220.

2. Some liberationists, such as Miranda, have convinced themselves that these are peripheral and inessential Marxist tenets, and that, strangely, Marx was himself actually a sort of Christian humanist. *See* José Porfirio Miranda, *Marx Against the Marxists: The Christian Humanism of Karl Marx* (Maryknoll, N.Y.: Orbis Books, 1980).

3. *See,* for example, Gustavo Gutiérrez "Expanding the View," 26. This essay first appeared in the fifteenth anniversary edition of his foundational work, *A Theology of Liberation*, published in 1988.

4. Karl Marx, letter to F. A. Sorge, Sept. 17, 1877, and to Wilhelm Liebknecht, Feb. 4, 1878. Dona Torr, ed., *Karl Marx and Friedrich Engels: Selected Correspondence*, 1846–1895, trans. Dona Torr (New York: International Publishers, 1942), 348, 357.

5. Peter Steinfels, "New Liberation Faith: Social Conflict is Muted," *New York Times*, July 27, 1988.

6. *See* Arthur F. McGovern, "Dependency Theory, Marxist Analysis, and Liberation Theology," in Ellis and Maduro, eds., *Expanding the View*, especially 87f. This essay first appeared in *The Future of Liberation Theology: Essays in Honor of Gustavo Gutiérrez* (Maryknoll, N.Y.: Orbis Books, 1989).

7. Lloyd D. Easton and Kurt H. Guddat, eds. and trans., *Writings of the Young Marx on Philosophy and Society* (Garden City, N.Y.: Doubleday Anchor Books, 1967), 11.

8. Karl Marx and Friedrich Engels, *The German Ideology*, in Easton and Guddat, eds., *Writings of the Young Marx*, 407, 409.

9. Karl Marx and Friedrich Engels, *The Communist Manifesto*, trans. Samuel Moore, in Lewis S. Feuer, ed., *Marx & Engels: Basic Writings on Politics & Philosophy* (Garden City, N.Y.: Doubleday, Anchor Books, 1959), especially 15–18, 20.

10. Karl Marx, *Economic and Philosophic Manuscripts of 1844*, trans. Martin Milligan, ed. Dirk J. Struik (New York: International Publishers, 1964), 107–15.

11. Karl Marx, *Capital* I, trans. Samuel Moore and Edward Aveling; rev. by Ernest Untermann according to the fourth German (1890) edition, Engels, ed. (New York: The Modern Library, copyright Charles H. Kerr & Co., 1906), 86, 126, 390 and *passim*; Marx and Engels, *The German Ideology*, in Easton and Guddat, eds., *Writings of the Young Marx*, 426.

12. *Capital* I, 196.

13. Karl Marx, *Critique of the Gotha Programme* (Moscow: Foreign Language Publishing House, n.d. but in accordance with the Russian *Gospolitizdat* edition of 1959), 22. Italics added.

14. Paul Craig Roberts and Matthew A. Stephenson, *Marx's Theory of Exchange, Alienation and Crisis* (Stanford, Calif.: Hoover Institution Press, 1973), 83.

15. *The German Ideology*, in Easton and Guddat, eds., *Writings of the Young Marx*, 425.

16. Ibid., 404.

17. *Capital* I, 534–35.

18. Nicholas Berdyaev, *The Meaning of the Creative Act*, trans. Donald A. Lowrie (New York: Collier Books, 1962), 9, 138.

19. Ronald H. Nash, *Poverty and Wealth* (Westchester, Ill.: Crossway Books, 1986), 94.

20. José Porfirio Miranda, *Communism in the Bible*, trans. Robert R. Barr (Maryknoll, N.Y.: Orbis Books, 1982), 6.

21. Gutiérrez, *A Theology of Liberation*, 91.

22. *Capital* I, 89.

23. Karl Marx, *Economic and Philosophic Manuscripts of 1844*, 78. Marx, *A Contribution to the Critique of Political Economy*, trans. S. W. Ryazanskaya, ed. Maurice Dobb (London: Lawrence & Wishart, 1971), 30.

24. *Capital* I, 232–33.

25. Ibid., 230–32.

26. Ibid., 568.

27. Ibid., 216.

28. Ibid.

29. Ibid., 645, 649, and *passim*.

30. In at least one place, this is tacitly recognized by Marx. He therein approvingly quotes, without any reservation, the following remark directed against J. B. Say by David Ricardo: "M. Say supposes, 'A landlord by his *assiduity, economy* and *skill*, to increase his annual revenue by 5,000 francs;' but a landlord has no means of employing his assiduity, economy and skill on his land, unless he farms it himself; and then it is in quality of capitalist and farmer that he makes the improvement, and not in quality of landlord. It is not conceivable that he could so augment the produce of his farm by any *peculiar* skill . ∴ on his part, without first increasing the quantity of capital employed upon it." Karl Marx, *Theories of Surplus Value, Capital* IV, 1862–63, trans. Emile Burns, ed. S. Ryazanskaya (Moscow: Foreign Languages Publishing House, n.d.), part II, 377. Italics added by Marx. Ellipses indicate a parenthetical interpolation by Marx that we have omitted for reasons of clarity, since it is not germane to the issue we address. From the context, it is evident that it is constant and not variable capital that is referred to here. Since nothing is said about the farmer employing workers, the application of capital enhances the productivity of his own current labor. If it did not do so in excess of the value of the past labor embodied in the capital, the farmer would have been better off consuming this value than investing it in further capital.

31. For Marx's contrary position, which amounts to little more than unsupported assertion, cf. *Capital* I, 425, note 1, and *Capital* III, F. Engels, ed. (Moscow: Foreign Languages Publishing House, 1959), chap. xlviii.

32. Karl Marx, *Pre-Capitalist Economic Foundations*, in the *Grundrisse der Kritik der Politischen Ökonomie*, trans. Jack Cohen, ed. E. J. Hobsbawm (London: Lawrence & Wishart, 1964), 107, 110–11, 113, 115; *Capital* I, 651, 787, 805, 815; *Capital* III, 792–801. Cf. *Capital* I, 623–24 for an apparent admission to the contrary, which is then discounted. *See also Capital* I, 637–40; and *Theories of Surplus Value* (*Capital* IV), part I, 59.

33. *Capital* I, 787–805; *Capital* III, 792, 801.

34. *Capital* III, 380.

35. Ibid., 103.

36. Letter to Joseph Weydemeyer, March 5, 1852, in Dona Torr, ed., *Marx-Engels Selected Correspondence* (New York: International Publishers, 1935), 57.

37. Gutiérrez, *The Power of the Poor in History*, 45. In Argentina this "clear-sighted segment" constituted the main power base of Juan Perón. Instead of availing himself of an unparalleled opportunity to institute wholesome structural change (by enacting, for example, policies in keeping with the spirit of Rivadavia's Law of Emphyteusis), Perón, although he subjected the landed oligarchy to threats, extortion, and humiliation, left its privileged structural position undisturbed.

38. Michael Novak, *Will It Liberate?*, 135f.

39. *"Zur Kritik der Hegelschen Rechtsphilosophie,"* quoted in Lichtheim, *Marxism*, 53.

40. Gutiérrez, "Pobres e Libertação em Puebla," *A Força Histórica dos Pobres*, trans. A. Cunha (Petrópolis: Vozes, 1984), 194–241; Jon Sobrino, *The True Church*

and the Poor, trans. Matthew J. O'Connell (Maryknoll, N.Y.: Orbis Books, 1984).

41. Reinhold Niebuhr, *An Interpretation of Christian Ethics* (New York: Harper, 1935), 118.

42. Ibid., 20.

43. Novak, *Will It Liberate?*, 117.

44. José Míguez Bonino, *Christians and Marxists* (Grand Rapids, Mich.: Eerdmans, 1976), 115.

45. McGovern, "Dependency Theory, Marxist Analysis, and Liberation Theology," 87f.

46. Steinfels, "New Liberation Faith."

47. Marx, *The Civil War in France* (Chicago: Charles H. Kerr & Co., 1934), 89.

48. Marx and Engels appropriated the term *communism* to distinguish their economic program from most rival socialist approaches. Engels, "Vorwort zur Broschure *Internationales aus dem 'Volkstaat' (1871–75)*" para. 7, quoted by Stanley Moore, *Marx on the Choice between Socialism and Communism* (Cambridge, Mass.: Harvard University Press, 1980), 2; preface to the 1888 English edition of *The Communist Manifesto*, in Feuer, ed., *Marx & Engels: Basic Writings*, 3f. They applied the term also to a few of the more extreme socialist systems, such as that of Weitling. In *State and Revolution* (New York: International Publishers, 1932), 76, 77, 81, Lenin canonized the practice among Marxist-Leninists of designating as socialism what Marx in his *Critique of the Gotha Programme* had called the first or lower phase of communist society. The ten measures outlined in *The Communist Manifesto* as "pretty generally applicable" in the "most advanced countries" "in the beginning" after the proletariat has gained political supremacy, are not presented as fully constituting even this lower phase, but are admittedly transitional expedients, intended to "outstrip themselves." Feuer, ed., *Marx & Engels: Basic Writings*, 28f.

49. Marx, *Critique of the Gotha Programme*, 20; Engels, *Anti-Dühring* (Moscow: Foreign Languages Publishing House, 1962), 423–25. Although written by Engels, *Anti-Dühring* was approved by Marx as representing their joint position.

50. Marx, *Critique of the Gotha Programme*, 20; *Capital* II, 434.

51. Marx, *Critique of the Gotha Programme*, 22.

52. Francois Noël ("Gracchus") Babeuf, *Pièces saises chez Babeuf* (Paris: Imprimarie Nationale, Nivose an V) II, 23. *See* Engels, *Anti-Dühring*, 425.

53. E.g., Gutiérrez, *A Theology of Liberation*, 31f.

54. Herbert Marcuse, *An Essay on Liberation* (Boston: Beacon Press, 1969), ix–x.

55. Ibid., 4.

56. Ibid., 87.

57. Ibid., 4.

58. Ibid., 90f.

59. Ibid., 89.

60. Ibid., 3–5.

61. Gutiérrez, *A Theology of Liberation*, 32.

62. McGovern, "Dependency Theory, Marxist Analysis, and Liberation Theology," pp. 83f. The statistics are cited from Michael P. Todaro, *Economic Development in the Third World*, 2d ed. (New York: Longman, 1981), 260.

63. Frank, *Capitalism and Underdevelopment in Latin America*, 3–6, 124ff., 146, 221–77, and *passim*.

64. Armen A. Alchian and William R. Allen, *University Economics*, 2d ed. (Belmont, Calif.: Wadsworth, 1967), 5.

65. Barbara Rudolph, "A Global Fire Sale," *Time* (April 22, 1991), 59f.

66. Novak, *Will It Liberate?*, 28, 58, 259f.

67. Howard J. Wiarda, quoted in *Will It Liberate?*, 260. Recognizing the bankruptcy of many of the policies initiated during his earlier terms in office, Paz Estenssoro instituted a program of sharp cutbacks in the public sector and greater reliance upon market forces. This program was further extended by the Paz Zamora administration that came into office in 1989. An annual inflation rate that exceeded 20,000 percent has been reduced to around 15 percent. The government deficit fell from 28 percent of gross domestic product to 6 percent. Instead of shrinking 23 percent annually, as it did during 1980–85, the economy has shown a modest positive growth rate. Information supplied by James L. Busey, political scientist specializing in Latin America, based on reports in standard Spanish-language and English-language sources.

68. Segundo, "Capitalism-Socialism: A Theological Crux," in Michael Novak, ed., *Liberation South/Liberation North*, 15.

69. *See*, for example, Miranda, *Communism in the Bible*, 3.

70. Segundo, "Capitalism-Socialism," in Novak, *Liberation South/Liberation North*, 15.

71. Ibid., 20. Question mark supplied.

72. William Temple, *Christianity and Social Order* (New York: Seabury, 1977; London: Shepheard-Walwyn, 1976), 65.

73. Insofar as its money supply is subject to manipulation by political appointees, this criticism may be applied to the United States which possesses, in that respect as well as others, a market system that is only relatively free.

74. From the comic strip, "The Wizard of Id," *Birmingham News*, April 18, 1988.

75. Ludwig von Mises, "Die Wirtschaftsrechnung im sozialistischen Gemeinwesen," *Archiv für Sozialwissenschaften* 47 (1920); trans. by S. Adler as "Economic Calculation in the Socialist Commonwealth," in F. A. Hayek, ed., *Collectivist Economic Planning*, (London: Routledge, 1935).

76. "The Case Against Liberation Theology," *The New York Times Magazine* (October 21, 1984), 51, 82–87, 93–95.

77. *See*, however, the contrary opinion by Harvey Cox, "Church Militant in Latin America," *Washington Post*, April 5, 1987, who cites many statements out of context and faults Novak for an emphasis which seems wholly proper to his announced purpose.

78. Most notably on 109–110.

79. Novak, *Will It Liberate?*, 172.

80. Ibid., 35, 85, 133, 134, 166, 306.

81. Ibid., 92.

82. Ibid., 81, 125, and *passim*.

83. Much the same criticism made here about Novak has been addressed to Paul E. Sigmond, *Liberation Theology at the Crossroads* (New York: Oxford University Press, 1990). In a review of his book, "The Church Is Still Restless," *New York Times*, April 14, 1990, Miriam Davidson writes that this book calls for a "third way—between capitalist exploitation and Marxist totalitarianism." But she complains, "Mr. Sigmund may also be guilty of the one thing for which he criticizes the

liberation theologians: not being sufficiently concrete in providing a prescription for a better society."

CHAPTER 8

1. Henry George, *Progress and Poverty*, book II, especially 104f., 111–113, and 137.

2. Donnella H. Meadows, Dennis L. Meadows, Jorgen Randers, and William W. Behrens III, *The Limits to Growth: A Report for the Club of Rome's Project on the Predicament of Mankind* (New York: Universe, 1972).

3. *Mater et Magistra* was delivered at St. Peter's in Rome, May 15, 1961. For the text, *see Seven Great Encyclicals*, 222–74. *Populorum Progressio* was delivered at St. Peter's in Rome, March 26, 1967. For the text, *see The Papal Encyclicals, 1958–1981* (Raleigh, N. Car.: McGrath Publishing Company, 1981), 183–201.

4. In this book "rent" and "land value" are used interchangeably according to established practice. However, a valid distinction may be made between the two: Physiocrats styled rent as that portion of the product that remains "after all the expenses of production that are resolvable into compensation for the exertion of individual labor are paid," and which is therefore attributable to land. Henry George, *The Science of Political Economy* (New York: Robert Schalkenbach Foundation, 1962), 150. Land value, on the other hand, is "the capitalized market price of private or misappropriated rent." W. A. Dowe, "Henry George's Errors," *Progress* (Melbourne), March, 1988, 2. Unlike rent, a value arising from production, land value stems from an institutionally recognized claim. If society did not recognize that claim, land value would disappear but rent would continue to exist.

5. Gaston Haxo, *The Philosophy of Freedom* (New York: Land and Freedom, 1941), 14.

6. Ibid., 50.

7. These widely accepted definitions stem from classical economics. Some economists subsume land under capital, call entrepreneurship a factor of production, and define taxes as another avenue of distribution, combining inherently unequal things and posing obstacles to clear analysis. As for Marx, he attacked the "trinity formula" of land-rent, capital-interest, and labor-wages as rationalizing "the interests of the ruling classes by proclaiming the physical necessity and eternal justification of their sources of revenue and elevating them into a dogma." *Capital* III, 797, 810.

8. George, *Progress and Poverty*, 166f.

9. These statistics are cited by Judith Hurley (with Kevin Daniher) in *Brazil: A Paradise Lost?* (San Francisco: Institute for Food and Development Policy, 1987), 3 and 1. The figures in the last sentence are from "Brazil's land reform program is caught in a violent crossfire," *Christian Science Monitor* (May 7, 1987), 19.

10. Alan B. Durning, "Brazil's Landless Lose Again," *World-Watch* (September–October, 1988), 9.

11. Cited in Hurley, 3, from "Brazil's land reform program . . . ," *Christian Science Monitor* (May 7, 1987), 11.

12. Some liberation theologians, drawing on the portrait of the early Church in the book of Acts, indicate that the distribution of goods should be based on need, rather than power. At the same time, however, Marcelo de Barros Souza, in *A Bíblia e a Luta Pela Terra*), 78–79 and the unnamed authors of the *Comentário aos*

Atos dos Apostolos (São Paulo: Edições Paulinas 1985), 35–36, in particular hold that the order of the early Christian society in Acts, based on sharing, is appropriate only to a voluntary fellowship and is not necessarily one that should be imposed upon society at large.

13. This is not to suggest that an individual cannot legitimately acquire material goods apart from the expenditure of his *own* labor, for full ownership includes the right of transfer through gift, bequest, and exchange.

14. John E. E. Dalberg Acton, *Essays on Freedom and Power* (Boston: Beacon Press, 1948), 12.

15. John Locke, *Second Treatise of Government*, chap. v, para. 34.

16. Ibid., para. 27.

17. George, *Progress and Poverty*, 347.

18. Ibid., 344–45.

19. Ibid., 365.

CHAPTER 9

1. It may not be necessary to say this, but if anyone should interpret our use of the biblical account of the conquest of Canaan as an apology for contemporary Israeli expansionism, he has altogether misunderstood what we are about.

2. Josephus, *Antiquities*, v. 76–78. According to Talmudic commentary in the *Gemara*, value was determined by location (distance from Jerusalem) as well as by fertility. Baba Batra 122, A.

3. Frederick Verinder, *My Neighbour's Landmark* (London: Land & Liberty Press, 1950), 39, 40.

4. Many Bible scholars hold that the Jubilee laws or the Sabbatical year laws were never fully implemented. *See* George A. Buttrick, ed. *The Interpreter's Dictionary of the Bible* (New York: Abingdon Press, 1962), II:1001–2; IV:141–44. But *cf.* Archer Torrey. *The Land and Biblical Economics*, 2nd ed. (New York: Henry George Institute, 1985).

5. Josephus, *Antiquities*, iii. 283–84.

6. *See* George R. Geiger, *The Philosophy of Henry George* (New York: Macmillan, 1933), 188 f.n.

7. Verinder, *My Neighbour's Landmark*, 77.

8. Ibid., 46.

9. E. R. A. Seligman, *Essays in Taxation*, 9th ed. (New York: Macmillan, 1923), chapt. 3.

10. Geiger, *The Philosophy of Henry George*, 108.

11. Ibid.

12. Seligman, *Essays in Taxation*, 81–83.

13. Jackson H. Ralston, *What's Wrong With Taxation?* (San Diego: Ingram Institute, 1932), 58.

14. Van Gogh sold but one painting during his entire lifetime. It was bought for 400 francs—the equivalent of slightly less than $1,400 in present-day purchasing power. A century later, his "Portrait of Dr. Gachet" fetched $82,500,000 at auction!

15. Winston S. Churchill, *The People's Rights* (New York: Taplinger, 1970), 118.

16. Winston S. Churchill, *Liberalism and the Social Problem* (London: Hodder & Stoughton, 1939), 318.

17. John R. Commons, *The Distribution of Wealth* (New York: Macmillan, 1893), 253.

18. Geiger, *The Philosophy of Henry George*, 260 f.n.

19. Marx, *Critique of the Gotha Programme*, 17.

20. Marx, *Capital* I, 835.

21. Ibid., 837.

22. Marx, *Capital* III, 800.

23. Marx, *Critique of the Gotha Programme*, 31.

24. Marx, "The Nationalization of the Land," a memorandum written for use by E. Dupont in making a speech on May 8, 1872, published as "The Abolition of Landed Property," with an erroneous editorial note, in Saul K. Padover, ed., *The Karl Marx Library* (New York: McGraw-Hill, 1973), III, 123. A version revised by Dupont was published under the first title in the *International Herald*, June 15, 1872, and is reprinted in vol. II of Marx's *Selected Works* (Moscow: Progress Publishers, 1973).

25. Marx, letter to Friedrich A. Sorge, dated June 30, 1881. Karl Marx and Frederick Engels, *Selected Correspondence*, trans. I. Lasker (Moscow: Progress Publishers, 1975), pp. 323f. *See also* Marx's much earlier rejection of proposals by Proudhon, J. S. Mill, and others, that "rent should be handed over to the state in place of taxes." *The Poverty of Philosophy* (New York: International Publishers, n.d.), 161.

26. " 'Each, giving himself to all gives himself to nobody': in other words, each gives himself to himself, and each is still his own master. The paradox conceals a paralogism. I surrender all myself—and I surrender it all to 999 others as well as myself; I only receive a fraction of the sovereignty of the community; and ultimately I must reflect that if I am the thousandth part of a tyrant, I am also the whole of a slave." Editor's introduction to Sir Ernest Barker, ed., *Social Contract: Essays by Locke, Hume, and Rousseau* (New York: Galaxy/Oxford University Press, 1962), xxxv.

27. George, *Progress and Poverty*, 405.

28. Louis Wasserman, in Andelson, *Critics of Henry George*, 36ff.

29. Steven B. Cord, in Andelson, *Critics of Henry George*, 184.

30. Henry George, "Thy Kingdom Come," a sermon delivered in Glasgow, 1889, and circulated in tract form by the Scottish Land Restoration League. Reprint ed. (New York: Robert Schalkenbach Foundation, n.d.).

31. Walter Rybeck, "The Property Tax as a Super User Charge," in C. Lowell Harriss, ed., *The Property Tax and Local Finance* (New York: Academy of Political Science, 1983), 133–47.

32. *See* George, *Progress and Poverty*, 420.

33. Ibid., 414.

34. Ibid., 418.

35. James L. Busey, in Andelson, *Critics of Henry George*, 331.

36. A. R. Hutchinson, *Natural Resources Rental Taxation in Australia*, 2d ed. (Melbourne: Land Values Research Group, n.d. but the figures reflect data through 1977), 31–32.

37. George, *Progress and Poverty*, 421.

38. Vance Packard, *The Hidden Persuaders* (New York: David McKay, 1957).

39. As university professors, we (the authors) would be hypocritical if we did not admit to some resentment of the disparity between our salaries and the incomes of rock stars, for example. But in a free market, individuals have the *opportunity* of making "best" choices. In a command economy, choices are made for them by

political functionaries whose judgment is no more infallible than their own. Even if given the power, we would be afraid to impose our "superior" value judgments upon the consuming public, lest we set a precedent that might lead others to impose their judgments upon us.

40. Maurice Allais, *Économie et Intérêt* (Paris: Imprimerie Nationale, 1947), 479, 499, 549, 566ff., and *passim. See also* another Nobel laureate in economics, Paul A. Samuelson, "Land and the Rate of Interest," in Harry I. Greenfield, et al., eds., *Theory for Economic Efficiency: Essays in Honor of Abba P. Lerner* (Cambridge, Ma.: MIT Press, 1979), 167-85.

41. Marx, *Critique of the Gotha Programme*, 20–22.

42. Les Hemingway, "Keeping Australia For Australians," *Good Government* (Sydney), August 1990, 7–8.

43. Fred Harrison, *The Power in the Land* (London: Shepheard-Walwyn, 1983), 168.

44. Reported by Marcus W. Brauchli and Masayoshi Kinabayashi, "Nervous Nippon," *Wall Street Journal*, 23 March 1990.

45. Ibid.

46. Ian Barron, "Adam Smith, Ricardo & the Case of Hong Kong," *Land & Liberty* (July–August, 1980), 59.

47. Reported in *The Public* (Chicago), 12 April, 1912.

48. Harrison, *The Power in the Land*, 227.

49. C. F. Koo, "Land Reform and Its Impact on Industrial Development in Taiwan," in J. R. Brown and Sein Lin, eds., *Land Reform in Developing Countries* (Hartford, Conn.: University of Hartford, 1968), 375.

50. A. R. Hutchinson, *Public Charges Upon Land Values*.

51. Hutchinson, *Natural Resources Rental Taxation in Australia* (Melbourne: Land Values Research Group, 1977), especially 18–19.

52. The February 1988 issue of the *National Geographic*, devoted to Australia's centennial, contained depressing photographs of slum properties in Sydney's Redfern district — scenes that seem to contradict what has been said above. "Reminiscent of New York City's South Bronx," read one caption, "this section of Redfern wears a facade of decay, graffiti its primary art form." However, the properties in question, consisting mainly of old row houses, had been purchased earlier by the government for use as Aboriginal low-income housing. So far as we have been able to determine, they are not subject to the site-value tax and its built-in incentives for upkeep and renewal.

53. R. W. Archer, *Site Value Taxation in Central Business District Redevelopment* (Washington, D.C.: Urban Land Institute, 1972), 24–37.

54. Rolland O'Regan, *Rating in New Zealand* (Wainuiomata, New Zealand: Baranduin Publishers, 1973), chap. IV.

55. *See* R. N. Carew Hunt, *The Theory and Practice of Communism*, 5th rev. ed. (New York: Macmillan, 1962), 127–28.

56. George, *Progress and Poverty*, 328.

57. Garrett Hardin, *Exploring New Ethics for Survival* (New York: Viking, 1972), 111, 116. Hardin's allegation is accepted here for purposes of discussion, although the evidence is mixed. His intention was not to establish a historical thesis although, at the time, he assumed the historical accuracy of his description. According to John Reader, the true common "was, by definition, an area of mutual benefit and responsibility, managed by those using it in a manner that acknowledged that envi-

ronmental resources are not unlimited." "Human Ecology: How Land Shapes Society," *New Scientist* 1629 (8 Sept., 1988), 51. Reader goes on to cite, among other instances, the Swiss alpine village of Törbel, which has maintained and managed a common in this sensitive manner for nearly a thousand years.

58. Garrett Hardin, "The Tragedy of the Commons," *Science* 162 (13 December 1968), 1243–48.

CHAPTER 10

1. George, *Progress and Poverty*, 552.
2. Within the community as well as within the individual.
3. Robert V. Andelson, *Imputed Rights*, 77–78.
4. Paulo Freire, *Pedagogy for the Oppressed* (New York: Herder and Herder, 1970).
5. An interesting connection with this struggle for land occurred 1,500 years later. In calling for the abolition of serfdom and the restoration of the common lands, the peasants in sixteenth-century Germany voiced demands which were logically implied by Luther's doctrine of the priesthood of all believers—that the service of God to which all the faithful are elected requires access to the land and its resources and the free disposal of one's person and of the product of one's toil. Despite the excesses which accompanied this Peasants' Revolt, Luther's part in the suppression of a movement which stemmed logically from his own teaching is a source of some pain to those who admire him for his spiritual genius and integrity.

APPENDIX

1. This sketch is based on the following principal sources: Henry George, Jr., *The Life of Henry George* (New York: Doubleday and McClure, 1900); Louis F. Post, *The Prophet of San Francisco* (New York: Vanguard Press, 1930); Anna George de Mille, *Henry George: Citizen of the World*, ed. Don C. Shoemaker (Chapel Hill, N. C.: University of North Carolina Press, 1950); Charles Albro Barker, *Henry George* (New York: Oxford University Press, 1955).
2. *Overland Monthly*, Oct. 1868. Quoted in Henry George, Jr., *The Life of Henry George*, 178f.
3. Quoted in ibid., 193 and 311.
4. Quoted in ibid., 210, from Ralph Meeker's unpublished "Notes on Conversations with Henry George" (Oct. 1897).
5. George, *Progress and Poverty*, 560.
6. Leo Tolstoy, "A Great Iniquity," London *Times*, August 1, 1905. Quoted in Geiger, *The Philosophy of Henry George*, 460.
7. From the flyleaf of Henry George, *Progresso e pobreza*, trans., Américo Werneck, Jr., 2d ed. (Rio de Janeiro: Gráfica Editora Aurora, Lta., 1946). Costa's statement rendered from Portuguese into English by James L. Busey.
8. Quoted in George, Jr., *Life of Henry George*, 321.
9. Archibald Henderson, *The Life of George Bernard Shaw* (Cincinnati: Stewart and Kidd, 1911). Quoted in Anna George de Mille, *Henry George: Citizen of the World*, 115.
10. From George's speech accepting the mayoralty nomination. Quoted in George, Jr., 467.

11. Quoted in ibid., 463.

12. Charles Edward Russell, *Bare Hands and Stone Walls* (New York: Scribners, 1933), 47. Quoted in Charles Albro Barker, *Henry George*, 480.

13. For a biography of Father McGlynn, *see* Stephen Bell, *Rebel, Priest and Prophet* (New York: Robert Schalkenbach Foundation, 1937).

14. Ibid., 44.

15. Post, *The Prophet of San Francisco*, 194.

16. *"Moses," A Lecture*, 1878 (New York: Robert Schalkenbach Foundation, n.d.), 9–10. The order of passages has been reversed in the quotation.

17. Joseph A. Schumpeter, *History of Economic Analysis*, ed., Elizabeth Boody Schumpeter (New York: Oxford University Press, 1954), 865.

18. John Bates Clark, *The Distribution of Wealth* (New York: Macmillan, 1899), viii.

19. The edition currently in print is part of a volume that contains four other works, including the text of *Rerum Novarum*. Henry George, *The Land Question* (New York: Robert Schalkenbach Foundation, 1984).

20. Quoted in Barker, *Henry George*, 576.

21. A letter to the New York *Times* from Dr. Henry Carey, one of McGlynn's devotees, implied a more cynical motive for the reinstatement. It claimed the excommunication had led to a drastic reduction, even as far away as South America, in the contributions to Peter's Pence—from which the Holy See was to a large extent sustained. Bell, *Rebel, Priest and Prophet*, 242. An arguably more compelling consideration was the fact that the excommunication had played into the hands of rabid anti-Catholics, giving them ammunition to charge that the Vatican, as a "foreign power," was interfering in American politics by dictating to American citizens (who happened to be Catholic laity or priests) what positions they should take on public issues.

22. Quoted in de Mille, *Henry George*, 229.

23. Quoted in George, Jr., *The Life of Henry George*, 605f.

24. Quoted in ibid., 605.

25. Quoted in de Mille, *Henry George*, 239.

General Index

(In some instances, especially where quotations are involved, the subjects listed in this index are not cited by name on the referenced page. For complete references, see the Notes.)

Scripture Index